Collectors' Coins - Decimal Issues of the United Kingdom

(Formerly <u>Check Your Change</u>)

By C H Perkins.

7th Edition © 2020

ISBN: 978-0-948964-99-2

This title is available as an eBook edition and some of it's price data is also part of the 'Check Your Change' app.

A comprehensive UK decimal coin catalogue with values, descriptions and photographs

Special thanks to Lee Holt for his tireless research, Sarah Grant, M McKerlie and others.

Errors and Omissions:

Every effort has been made to ensure that the information and price data contained within this book are accurate and complete. However, errors do sometimes have a habit of creeping in unnoticed, and with this in mind the following email address has been established for notifications of omissions and errors: info@coinpublications. com. Readers within the UK can also call the telephone number below.

COIN
PUBLICATIONS

coinpublications.com
020 308 69996

TABLE OF CONTENTS

INTRODUCTION

Welcome to the "Collectors' Coins - Decimal Issues of the UK" 2020 edition.

This inexpensive book, with listings and colour pictures of every circulated decimal coin type (and a lot more) should provide an excellent guide to modern coinage and as such, should aid existing collectors and hopefully stimulate new ones.

Decimal coinage first appeared fifty-two years ago and has become increasingly popular over the last few years. People want authoritative information without the urban myths, rumours and influence of media hype. This book has evolved over more than fifty years to provide that information.

NEW IN 2020

The book is a bit late this year. To be honest, it's only partly due to the terrible corona-virus pandemic, and more a lack of motivation on my part! Every time I thought I was up-to-date and well informed on the latest issues the Royal Mint decided to churn out another load of new gimmicky 'coins' that will never appear in circulation and can only be bought in packs or sets. Some people still feel the need to own them all but increasingly there are grumblings about it all being rather too much, and too expensive. The fact that there aren't all that many new coins you can actually find for 'free' in your change is also disheartening to many collectors.

The corona-virus has - at the time of writing - lead to a lull in the production of new coin issues and also some stagnation in buying and selling on the second hand market - in fact I took the decision on the 23rd March to suspend all buying / selling / swapping of coins on my Facebook group 'Check Your Change, UK decimal coins info, swap and trade' group, as there really are more important things that need to be delivered than coins and people shouldn't need to venture out to post them to people. For me personally, working from home as ever, it's an ideal opportunity to get this book finished and to concentrate on making it the biggest and best ever. This book contains twelve more pages than the previous edition.

Apart from the new coins and many updated valuations, the biggest change this year is probably my decision to do away with the confusing 'BU' term and replace it with 'As-New', which brings it in-line with the 'Check Your Change' app - more on that on page 5.

Please do have a look at my website, which is optimised for smart-phones and contains details of all the half penny to £5 coins made since 1968:

www.checkyourchange.co.uk

This book also has its own large Facebook group:
Search there for 'Check Your Change'.
For details on the Check Your Change app to aid cataloguing your coins see p.82.

Thank-you to each and every book owner, group member and app user for your support of Check Your Change!

Stay safe, stay healthy! C H Perkins, mid May 2020.

USING THIS CATALOGUE

The values listed in this catalogue are the result of many hours of compiling and comparing sale prices from a few sources. For some items, there is such a limited number of transactions on which to base the values that they may seem conservative. Others may seem to high - remember, all coins are essentially worth what someone else willing to pay for them, and that worth can change fairly quickly.

For coins that have consistent extra value in used condition, a 'Used' value is shown. Sometimes other coins can sell for more than face value in 'Used' condition, it all depends on how badly someone needs it and how much they are willing to pay for the convenience of not having to go through their own change to find one.

MINTAGES

The numbers given as mintages are based on information available from many sources, including other reference works, online sources, and the Royal Mint. The accuracy of these numbers is by no means guaranteed, and modifications may be made as better information becomes available. It should also be noted that for some of the most recent special issues, the mintages given are the "maximum mintages", and the actual number of pieces struck may be currently unknown. Again, updates will be made when new information is available.

COIN GRADES

The listings in this catalogue contain three or four values, where applicable. These are as follows:

Used - A coin from circulation with normal wear and the usual bumps and scrapes from use. Most coins are just worth face value in used condition but for those that consistently sell for more than face value a 'Used' value is shown.

Uncirculated (UNC) - Appears as it did when it left the Mint. There will be no signs of wear or handling. It may show minimal "bag marks", as is common for mass-produced coins. Should be free of other major faults - and in an ideal world you'd also expect the dies that were used to strike the coin to have been in good condition and free of signs of excessive use.

As-New (formerly 'BU') - A coin in as-new condition with full or virtually full mint-lustre, i.e. brilliance. For older decimal coins, pre approx 2002-ish it is possible (but fairly hard) to find very well kept circulation issue coins that are practically flawless and what I would deem 'as-new' - with excellent surfaces and full mint lustre. In fact some older circulation coins seem to be of higher quality than the coins the Royal Mint currently sell in their BU packaging (manufacturing standards were considerably higher then)! More recent coins struck to the Royal Mint 'Brilliant Uncirculated' standard (without any damage or signs of use) can also be considered 'as-new' in most cases.

Proof - A coin struck from specially prepared coin dies on a specially pre-pared metal blank. Because of this extra care, Proofs usually exhibit much sharper detail and have mirror-like blank flat areas (technically called the 'fields'). Some proof coins show frosted design details and such coins with contrasting raised design elements and mirror-like fields are sometimes called 'cameo', a term which originated in the USA.

THE VALUE OF GOLD

The price of gold influences the gold coin prices quoted in this book. The prices quoted here are based on a gold value of about £1,360 per ounce or £43,800 per kilogramme.

What's currently legal tender?

No half pennies are legal tender. They were demonetised on the 31st December 1984. Banks do accept them, but the high street financial institutions are not exactly falling over themselves to exchange the half-pee and many will likely refuse them.

Which are hard to find?

The 1972 coin was made as a proof only and was only included in proof sets, so is harder to find. The last coin, dated 1984 was also made for proof and BU sets only.

OBVERSE

OBVERSE 1
(used 1971 - 1984)
D•G•REG•F•D•(date) || ELIZABETH II
Elizabeth II, Dei Gratia Regina, Fidei Defensor
(Elizabeth II, By the Grace of God Queen and Defender of the Faith)
Portrait by: Arnold Machin

REVERSES

REVERSE 1
(used 1971 - 1981)
Regal Crown
$^1/_2$ NEW PENNY
Design by: Christopher Ironside

REVERSE 2
(used 1982 - 1984)
Regal Crown
$^1/_2$ HALF PENNY
Design by: Christopher Ironside

INFO

Although it was known from the onset that the half-penny would see limited circulation, it was necessary to help facilitate the transition from 'old money' to decimal, as the old sixpence coins were still circulating as 2½ new pence.

TYPE 1 (obverse 1, reverse 1)

Year	Mintage	UNC	As-New	Proof
1971	1,394,188,250	£0.20	£0.50	£2.00
1972	Proof Only	Used: £1.00		£5.00
1973	365,680,000	£0.20	£1.00	£2.00
1974	365,448,000	£0.20	£1.00	£2.00
1975	197,600,000	£0.20	£1.00	£2.00
1976	412,172,000	£0.20	£1.00	£2.00
1977	86,368,000	£0.20	£1.00	£2.00
1978	59,532,000	£0.20	£1.00	£2.00
1979	219,132,000	£0.20	£1.00	£2.00
1980	202,788,000	£0.20	£1.00	£2.00
1981	46,748,000	£0.20	£1.00	£2.00

TYPE 2 (obverse 1, reverse 2)

Year	Mintage	UNC	As-New	Proof
1982	190,752,000	£0.20	£1.00	£2.00
1983	7,600,000	£0.20	£1.00	£2.00
1984	158,820 [‡2]	Used: £1.00	£5.00	£5.00

NOTES

[‡2] This year was not issued for circulation, and the "business strikes" were made for BU sets, only.

What's currently legal tender?

All 1p coins are legal tender. Merchants are allowed by law to refuse payments made in 1p or 2p coins if the combined total value of the 'coppers' is more than 20p in any one transaction.

Which are hard to find?

1972 coins were made as proofs only and were only included in proof sets, so is not likely to be found in circulation. In 1992 the alloy was changed from bronze to copper-plated steel. In that year both types exist and the bronze (non magnetic) 1992 coin is not usually found in circulation. Both bronze and copper-plated steel coins also exist for 1999, with the bronze coins distributed just within the year sets. See the end of this penny section for details on portcullis reverse varieties.

OBVERSES

OBVERSE 1
(used 1971 - 1984)
D•G•REG•F•D•(date) || ELIZABETH II
Elizabeth II, Dei Gratia Regina, Fidei Defensor
(Elizabeth II, By the Grace of God Queen and Defender of the Faith)
Portrait by: Arnold Machin

OBVERSE 2
(used 1985 - 1997)
ELIZABETH II || D•G•REG•F•D•(date)
Elizabeth II, Dei Gratia Regina, Fidei Defensor
(Elizabeth II, By the Grace of God Queen and Defender of the Faith)
Portrait by: Raphael Maklouf

OBVERSE 3
(used 1998 - 2008)
ELIZABETH•II•D•G || REG•F•D•(date)
Elizabeth II, Dei Gratia Regina, Fidei Defensor
(Elizabeth II, By the Grace of God Queen and Defender of the Faith)
Portrait by: Ian Rank-Broadley

OBVERSE 4 (similar to last, with no rim beading)
(used 2008 - 2015)
ELIZABETH•II•D•G || REG•F•D•(date)
Elizabeth II, Dei Gratia Regina, Fidei Defensor
(Elizabeth II, By the Grace of God Queen and Defender of the Faith)
Portrait by: Ian Rank-Broadley

OBVERSE 5
(used 2015 onwards)
ELIZABETH II•DEI•GRA•REG•FID•DEF•(date)
Elizabeth II, Dei Gratia Regina, Fidei Defensor
(Elizabeth II, By the Grace of God Queen and Defender of the Faith)
Portrait by: Jody Clark

20.32 mm • 3.56 grammes • bronze • plain edge

REVERSES

REVERSE 1
(used 1971 - 1981)
Crowned portcullis
[A portcullis with chains royally crowned]
1 NEW PENNY
Design by: Christopher Ironside

REVERSE 2
(used 1982 - 2008 and for 2018 silver pennies)
Crowned portcullis
[A portcullis with chains royally crowned]
1 ONE PENNY
Design by: Christopher Ironside

REVERSE 3
(used 2008 to date)
Lower left section of the Royal coat of Arms of the
United Kingdom.
ONE PENNY
Design by: Matthew Dent

TYPE 1 (obverse 1, reverse 1)

		UNC	As-New	Proof
1971	1,521,666,250	£0.10	£0.20	£2.00
1972	Proof Only (from the sets)	Used: £1.00		£6.00
1973	280,196,000	£0.20	£1.00	£4.00
1974	330,892,000	£0.20	£1.00	£3.00
1975	221,604,000	£0.20	£1.00	£3.00
1976	300,160,000	£0.20	£1.00	£3.00
1977	285,430,000	£0.20	£1.00	£3.00
1978	292,770,000	£0.20	£1.00	£3.00
1979	459,000,000	£0.20	£1.00	£3.00
1980	416,304,000	£0.20	£1.00	£3.00
1981	301,800,000	£0.20	£1.00	£3.00

TYPE 2 (obverse 1, reverse 2)

		UNC	As-New	Proof
1982	100,292,000	£0.20	£1.00	£4.00
1983	243,002,000	£0.20	£1.00	£4.00
1984	154,759,625	£0.20	£2.00	£3.00

20.32 mm • 3.56 grammes • bronze/cu plated • plain edge

TYPE 3 (obverse 2, reverse 2)

				UNC	As-New	Proof
1985	200,605,245			£0.20	£2.00	£3.00
1986	369,989,130			£0.20	£2.00	£3.00
1987	499,946,000			£0.20	£2.00	£3.00
1988	793,492,000			£0.20	£2.00	£3.00
1989	658,142,000			£0.20	£2.00	£3.00
1990	529,047,500			£0.20	£2.00	£3.00
1991	206,457,600			£0.20	£2.00	£3.00
1992	78,421	‡	Bronze	£3.00	£5.00	£5.00

TYPE 4 (obverse 2, reverse 2)
From now on, made of copper-plated steel (which is slightly magnetic)

		UNC	As-New	Proof
1992	253,867,000	£0.10	£2.00	-
1993	602,590,000	£0.10	£2.00	£3.00
1994	843,834,000	£0.10	£2.00	£3.00
1995	303,314,000	£0.10	£2.00	£3.00
1996	723,840,060	£0.10	£2.00	£3.00
1997	396,874,000	£0.10	£2.00	£3.00

TYPE 5 (obverse 3, reverse 2)

			UNC	As-New	Proof
1998	739,770,000		£0.10	£2.00	£3.00
1999	891,392,000	(‡ also in bronze)		£2.00	£3.00
2000	1,060,364,000		£0.10	£2.00	£3.00
2001	928,802,000		£0.10	£2.00	£3.00
2002	601,446,000		£0.10	£2.00	£3.00
2003	539,436,000		£0.10	£2.00	£3.00
2004	739,764,000		£0.10	£2.00	£3.00
2005	536,318,000		£0.10	£2.00	£3.00
2006	524,605,000		£0.10	£2.00	£3.00
2007	548,002,000		£0.10	£2.00	£3.00
2008	180,600,000		£0.10	£2.00	£3.00

TYPE 6 (obverse 4, reverse 3)

		UNC	As-New	Proof
2008 ‡2	507,952,000	FV	£2.00	£3.00
2009	556,412,800	FV	£2.00	£3.00
2010	609,603,000	FV	£2.00	£3.00
2011	431,004,000	FV	£2.00	£3.00
2012	227,201,000	FV	£2.00	£3.00
2013	260,800,000	FV	£2.00	£4.00
2014	464,801,520	FV	£2.00	£4.00
2015	154,600,000	FV	£2.00	£4.00

TYPE 7 (obverse 5, reverse 3)

			UNC	As-New	Proof
2015	418,201,016		FV	£3.00	£5.00
2016	368,482,000		FV	£3.00	£5.00
2017	240,990,600		FV	£3.00	£4.00
2018	Not yet known	Currently in sets only		£3.00	£5.00
2019	Not yet known	Currently in sets only		£3.00	£5.00
2020	Not yet known	Currently in sets only		£2.00	£4.00

Special Sterling Silver Coins (Type 6 to 2015)

Sterling Silver pennies struck by the Royal Mint and available with pouches, marketed as gifts for new born babies from 2009 onwards.

			BU
1996	Unknown	Silver coin, originally part of a set	£20.00
2009	8,467	All below prices inc. original packaging	£15.00
2010	9,701		£15.00
2011			£15.00
2012	5,548		£15.00
2013	8,920	Plus 1,679 definitive silver pennies?	£14.00
2014 & 2015		Royal Mint, price new	£30.00
2016	Type 7	Royal Mint, price new	£30.00
2017	Type 7	Royal Mint, price new	£30.00
2018	Reverse 2	Royal Mint, price new (2 pack types)	£15/£30
2019/2020 Reverse 2, w/date below		Royal Mint, price new	£15.00

NOTES

[1] In 1992, a change in alloy was made from bronze to copper-plated steel. In 1992 the original bronze planchets were only used for the BU Mint folders and Proof sets. The copper-plated steel planchets were used for circulation strikes only. The same thing happened in 1999 when bronze blanks were used in proof and BU sets.

[2] The Dent reverse 2008 1p has been reported to exist with 180 degree (inverted) die alignment.

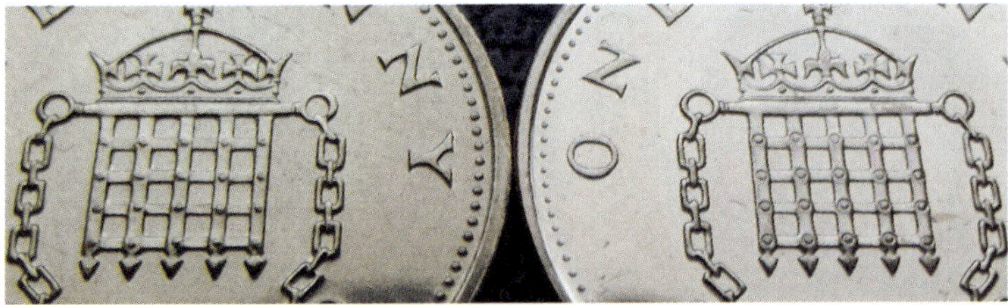

There are varieties of 1p coins that concern the rivets on the portcullis. It seems that for some years the coins in the BU sets (and proofs) were struck using different dies, resulting in two different types. Both types of rivets (either circles as shown in the right image or dots as seen in the left image) occur for the following portcullis reverse coins:
1986, 1988, 1989, 1990, 1992, 1993, 2007, 2008.

What's currently legal tender?

All 2p coins are legal tender. Merchants are allowed by law to refuse payments made in 1p or 2p coins if the combined total value of the 'coppers' is more than 20p in any one transaction.

Which are hard to find?

The change from using bronze to using copper-plated steel has led to a couple of scarcer types - The 1992 coin made of bronze (i.e. non magnetic) is much scarcer than the 1992 coin made of copper-plated steel. Bronze and copper-plated steel were also used in 1998, although both types seem fairly common.

By far the rarest and most expensive 2p is the 1983 error coin, which has 'NEW PENCE' on the reverse, instead of 'TWO PENCE'. This mistake just affects the 1983 2p; no other dates are affected. The error coins went into some BU sets and were not generally circulated. It is possible though, that some of the sets were broken up before the error was known about, so there may be a few very rare 2p coins out there, in fact one or two have apparently turned up in change!

OBVERSES

OBVERSE 1
(used 1971 - 1984)
D•G•REG•F•D•(date) || ELIZABETH II
Elizabeth II, Dei Gratia Regina, Fidei Defensor
(Elizabeth II, By the Grace of God Queen and Defender of the Faith)
Portrait by: Arnold Machin

OBVERSE 2
(used 1985 - 1997)
ELIZABETH II || D•G•REG•F•D•(date)
Elizabeth II, Dei Gratia Regina, Fidei Defensor
(Elizabeth II, By the Grace of God Queen and Defender of the Faith)
Portrait by: Raphael Maklouf

OBVERSE 3
(used 1998 - 2008)
ELIZABETH•II•D•G || REG•F•D•(date)
Elizabeth II, Dei Gratia Regina, Fidei Defensor
(Elizabeth II, By the Grace of God Queen and Defender of the Faith)
Portrait by: Ian Rank-Broadley

OBVERSE 4 (similar to last, with no rim beading)
(used 2008 - 2015)
ELIZABETH•II•D•G || REG•F•D•(date)
Elizabeth II, Dei Gratia Regina, Fidei Defensor
(Elizabeth II, By the Grace of God Queen and Defender of the Faith)
Portrait by: Ian Rank-Broadley

OBVERSES - continued

OBVERSE 5
(used 2015 onwards)
ELIZABETH II•DEI•GRA•REG•FID•DEF•(date)
Elizabeth II, Dei Gratia Regina, Fidei Defensor
(Elizabeth II, By the Grace of God Queen and Defender of the Faith)
Portrait by: Jody Clark

REVERSES

REVERSE 1
(used 1971 - 1981 and for the error 1983 coin)
Plumes in Coronet
[OFFICIALLY: The Badge of the Prince of Wales, with his
motto ICH DIEN]
2 NEW PENCE
Design by: Christopher Ironside

REVERSE 2
(used 1982 - 2008)
Plumes in Coronet
[OFFICIALLY: The Badge of the Prince of Wales, with his
motto ICH DIEN]
2 TWO PENCE
Design by: Christopher Ironside

REVERSE 3
(used 2008 to date)
Upper right section of the Royal coat of Arms of
the United Kingdom.
TWO PENCE
Design by: Matthew Dent

INFO

The current minting facility at Llantrisant,
Mid Glamorgan, was built in 1967 in order to meet
the demand for the millions of coins needed
for the conversion to the modern decimal
system now used in the United Kingdom.

25.91 mm • 7.13 grammes • bronze • plain edge

TYPE 1 (obverse 1, reverse 1)

			UNC	As-New	Proof
1971	1,454,856,250		£0.10	£0.30	£2.00
1972		Proof Only (from the sets) Used: £2.00			£10.00
1973		Proof Only (from the sets) Used: £2.00			£10.00
1974		Proof Only (from the sets) Used: £2.00			£10.00
1975	145,545,000		£0.30	£1.00	£2.00
1976	181,379,000		£0.30	£1.00	£3.00
1977	109,281,000		£0.30	£1.00	£2.00
1978	189,658,000		£0.30	£1.00	£2.00
1979	260,200,000		£0.30	£1.00	£2.00
1980	408,527,000		£0.30	£1.00	£2.00
1981	353,191,000		£0.30	£1.00	£3.00

TYPE 2 (obverse 1, reverse 2)

			UNC	As-New	Proof
1982	205,000	[1]	Used: £1.00	£5.00	£8.00
1983	631,000	[1]	Used: £1.00	£5.00	£8.00
1983	Error, 'NEW PENCE' reverse	Used: £400 - £600	£1k - £1.2k		
1984	158,820	[1]	Used: £1.00	£5.00	£6.00

TYPE 3 (obverse 2, reverse 2)

			UNC	As-New	Proof
1985	107,113,000		£0.50	£2.00	£3.00
1986	168,967,500		£0.50	£2.00	£3.00
1987	218,100,750		£0.50	£2.00	£3.00
1988	419,889,000		£0.50	£2.00	£3.00
1989	359,226,000		£0.50	£2.00	£3.00
1990	204,499,700		£0.50	£2.00	£3.00
1991	86,625,000		£0.50	£2.00	£3.00
1992	78,421	[2] Bronze	Used: £1.00	£5.00	£3.00

NOTES

There are some very subtle 2p 'micro varieties'.

[1] These years were not issued for circulation, and the "business strikes" were made for BU mint folders, only.

[2] In 1992, a change in alloy was made from bronze to copper-plated steel. The original bronze blanks were only used for the BU Mint folders and Proof sets. The copper-plated steel blanks were used for circulation strikes only.

[3] In 1998, both bronze and copper-plated steel blanks were used. It is estimated that about 55% of the mintage was bronze.

[4] In 1999, bronze blanks were used for Proof and BU sets.

[5] A proof silver 1996 2p exists, it was originally available in a set.

TYPE 4 (obverse 2, reverse 2) From now on, made of copper-plated steel (slightly magnetic)

			UNC	As-New	Proof
1992	102,247,000		£0.20	£2.00	-
1993	235,674,000		£0.20	£2.00	£2.00
1994	531,628,000		£0.20	£2.00	£3.00
1995	124,482,000		£0.20	£2.00	£3.00
1996	296,276,000 ‡5		£0.20	£2.00	£3.00
1997	496,116,000		£0.20	£2.00	£3.00

TYPE 5 (obverse 3, reverse 2)

			UNC	As-New	Proof
1998	231,830,000 ‡3	Copper / Steel	£0.20	£2.00	£3.00
1998	About 55% of total ‡3	Bronze	£0.20	£2.00	
1999	353,816,000	Copper / Steel	£0.20	£2.00	£3.00
1999	‡4	Bronze Proof			£4.00
2000	583,643,000		£0.20	£2.00	£3.00
2001	551,886,000		£0.20	£2.00	£3.00
2002	168,556,000		£0.20	£2.00	£3.00
2003	260,225,000		£0.20	£2.00	£3.00
2004	356,396,000		£0.20	£2.00	£3.00
2005	280,396,000		£0.20	£2.00	£3.00
2006	170,637,000		£0.20	£2.00	£3.00
2007	254,500,000		£0.20	£2.00	£4.00
2008	10,600,000				

TYPE 6 (obverse 4, reverse 3)

			UNC	As-New	Proof
2008	241,679,000		£0.20	£2.00	£4.00
2009	150,500,500		£0.20	£2.00	£3.00
2010	99,600,000		£0.20	£2.00	£3.00
2011	114,300,000		£0.20	£2.00	£3.00
2012	67,800,000		FV	£2.00	£4.00
2013	40,600,000		FV	£2.00	£5.00
2014	247,600,020		FV	£2.00	£5.00
2015	85,900,000		FV	£2.00	£5.00

TYPE 7 (obverse 5, reverse 3)

			UNC	As-New	Proof
2015	139,200,000		FV	£2.00	£6.00
2016	185,660,000		FV	£4.00	£6.00
2017	16,600,000		FV	£4.00	£6.00
2018	Not yet known	Currently in sets only.		£4.00	£6.00
2019	Not yet known	Currently in sets only.		£4.00	£6.00
2020	Not yet known	Currently in sets only.		£4.00	£6.00

What's currently legal tender?
Only the smaller post-1990 5p coins are legal tender. The older large coins can be paid into UK bank accounts at face value. The predecessor of the five pence, the shilling, should also be accepted at most UK banks as five pence. Check any shillings have no collectable worth using the Coin Publications book "Collectors' Coins GB 1760 - 1970" before redeeming them at five pence face value.

Which are hard to find?
The old large 5p coins are no longer found in change (unless someone has managed to pass one off as a 10p, which sometimes happens). The scarcest are those that were made just to go into sets, or as proofs only: notably 1972 to 1974, 1976, a few of the early and mid 1980s coins, and the last large 5p struck in 1990. From 2012 onwards the 5p is made of nickel-plated steel and is magnetic.

OBVERSES

OBVERSE 1
(used 1968 - 1984)
D•G•REG•F•D•(date) || ELIZABETH II
Elizabeth II, Dei Gratia Regina, Fidei Defensor
(Elizabeth II, By the Grace of God Queen and Defender of the Faith)
Portrait by: Arnold Machin

OBVERSE 2
(used 1985 - 1990)
ELIZABETH II || D•G•REG•F•D•(date)
Elizabeth II, Dei Gratia Regina, Fidei Defensor
(Elizabeth II, By the Grace of God Queen and Defender of the Faith)
Portrait by: Raphael Maklouf

REVERSES

REVERSE 1
(used 1968 - 1981)
Crowned Thistle
[OFFICIALLY: The Badge of Scotland, a thistle royally crowned]
5 NEW PENCE
Design by: Christopher Ironside

REVERSE 2
(used 1982 - 1990)
Crowned Thistle
[OFFICIALLY: The Badge of Scotland, a thistle royally crowned]
5 FIVE PENCE
Design by: Christopher Ironside

TYPE 1 (obverse 1, reverse 1)

Year	Mintage		UNC	As-New	Proof
1968	98,868,250		£0.30	£1.00	
1969	120,270,000		£0.50	£2.00	
1970	225,948,525		£0.50	£2.00	
1971	81,783,475		£0.50	£2.00	£3.00
1972	Proof Only (from sets)	Used: £1.00			£6.00
1973	Proof Only (from sets)	Used: £1.00			£6.00
1974	Proof Only (from sets)	Used: £1.00			£6.00
1975	141,539,000		£0.50	£2.00	£3.00
1976	Proof Only (from sets)	Used: £1.00			£6.00
1977	24,308,000		£0.50	£2.00	£3.00
1978	61,094,000		£0.50	£2.00	£3.00
1979	155,456,000		£0.50	£2.00	£3.00
1980	220,566,000		£0.50	£2.00	£3.00
1981	Proof Only (from sets)	Used: £1.00			£6.00

TYPE 2 (obverse 1, reverse 2)

Year	Mintage		UNC	As-New	Proof
1982	205,000 ‡	Used: £1.00	£3.00	£6.00	£4.00
1983	631,000 ‡	Used: £1.00	£3.00	£5.00	£6.00
1984	158,820 ‡	Used: £1.00	£3.00	£5.00	£6.00

TYPE 3 (obverse 2, reverse 2)

Year	Mintage		UNC	As-New	Proof
1985	178,000 ‡	Used: £1.00	£3.00	£5.00	£5.00
1986	167,000 ‡	Used: £1.00	£3.00	£5.00	£5.00
1987	48,220,000		£1.00	£3.00	£3.00
1988	120,744,610		£1.00	£3.00	£3.00
1989	101,406,000		£1.00	£3.00	£3.00
1990	102,606 ‡	Used: £2.00	£3.50	£5.00	£4.00

NOTES

‡ These years were not issued for circulation, and the "business strikes" were made for BU mint folders, only.

INFO

As of December 31st 1990, the large five-pence coins were demonetised.

OBVERSES

OBVERSE 3
(used 1990 - 1997)
ELIZABETH II || D•G•REG•F•D•(date)
Elizabeth II, Dei Gratia Regina, Fidei Defensor
(Elizabeth II, By the Grace of God Queen and Defender of the Faith)
Portrait by: Raphael Maklouf

OBVERSE 4
(used 1998 - 2008)
ELIZABETH II•D•G || REG•F•D•(date)
Elizabeth II, Dei Gratia Regina, Fidei Defensor
(Elizabeth II, By the Grace of God Queen and Defender of the Faith)
Portrait by: Ian Rank-Broadley

OBVERSE 5 (similar to last, with no rim beading)
(used 2008 - 2015)
ELIZABETH II•D•G || REG•F•D•(date)
Elizabeth II, Dei Gratia Regina, Fidei Defensor
(Elizabeth II, By the Grace of God Queen and Defender of the Faith)
Portrait by: Ian Rank-Broadley

OBVERSE 6
(used 2015 onwards)
ELIZABETH II•DEI•GRA•REG•FID•DEF•(date)
Elizabeth II, Dei Gratia Regina, Fidei Defensor
(Elizabeth II, By the Grace of God Queen and Defender of the Faith)
Portrait by: Jody Clark

REVERSES

REVERSE 3
(used 1990 - 2008)
Crowned Thistle
[OFFICIALLY: The Badge of Scotland, a thistle royally crowned]
5 FIVE PENCE
Design by: Christopher Ironside

REVERSE 4
(used 2008 to date)
Middle part of the Royal coat of Arms of the United Kingdom.
FIVE PENCE
Design by: Matthew Dent

TYPE 4 - Reduced in size from 23.59mm to 18mm (obverse 3, reverse 3)

			UNC	As-New	Proof
1990	1,634,976,005	Edge varieties	£1.00	£3.00	£3.00
		1990 silver proof pair, Type 3 and Type 4			£22.00
1991	724,979,000		£1.00	£3.00	£3.00
1992	453,173,500		£1.00	£3.00	£3.00
1993	56,945 ‡1	Used: £1.00 £3.00		£6.00	£7.00
1994	93,602,000		£1.00	£3.00	£3.00
1995	183,384,000		£1.00	£3.00	£3.00
1996	302,902,000	(exists in silver)	£1.00	£3.00	£3.00
1997	236,596,000		£1.00	£3.00	£3.00

TYPE 5 (obverse 4, reverse 3)

			UNC	As-New	Proof
1998	217,376,000	100,000 proofs	£1.00	£3.00	£3.00
1999	195,490,000		£1.00	£3.00	£3.00
2000	388,506,000		£1.00	£3.00	£3.00
2001	320,330,000		£1.00	£3.00	£3.00
2002	219,258,000		£1.00	£3.00	£3.00
2003	333,230,000		£1.00	£3.00	£3.00
2004	271,810,000		£1.00	£3.00	£3.00
2005	236,212,000		£1.00	£3.00	£3.00
2006	317,697,000		£1.00	£3.00	£3.00
2007	246,720,000		£1.00	£3.00	£3.00
2008	92,880,000		£1.00	£3.00	£3.00

TYPE 6 (obverse 5, reverse 4, Nickel plated steel from 2012 onwards)

		UNC	As-New	Proof
2008	165,172,000 ‡2	£1.00	£4.00	£4.00
2009	132,960,300	£1.00	£4.00	£4.00
2010	396,245,500	£1.00	£4.00	£4.00
2011	50,400,000	£1.00	£4.00	£4.00
2012	339,802,350	£1.00	£4.00	£4.00
2013	378,800,750	£1.00	£4.00	£4.00
2014	885,004,520	£1.00	£4.00	£4.00
2015	163,000,000	£1.00	£4.00	£4.00

TYPE 7 (obverse 6, reverse 4)

			UNC	As-New	Proof
2015	536,600,000		FV	£4.00	£4.00
2016	305,740,000		FV	£4.00	£4.00
2017	220,515,000		FV	£4.00	£4.00
2018	Not yet known	Currently in sets only		£4.00	£4.00
2019	Not yet known			£4.00	£4.00
2020	Not yet known	Currently in sets only		£4.00	£4.00

‡1   1993 was not issued for circulation, and the "business strikes" were made for BU mint folders, only.

‡2   The Dent reverse 2008 5p has been reported to exist with incorrect die alignment of up to 180 degrees!

19

What's currently legal tender?

Only the smaller post-1992 10p coins are legal tender. The older large coins can be paid into UK bank accounts. The predecessor of the ten pence, the florin or two-shillings, should also be accepted at most UK banks. Check any florins have no collectable worth using the Coin Publications book "Collectors' Coins GB 1760 - 1970" before redeeming them at ten pence face value.

Which are hard to find?

The rarest 10p is the 2009 coin with the wrong (previous type) reverse! Only two or three of these are known so far and it is thought that they were included erroneously in some baby gift sets - it's certainly one that can easily be overlooked. The old large 10p coins are no longer found in change. The scarcest of those were made just to go into sets, or as proofs: notably 1972, 1978 and all of the large type coins from 1982 onwards. The alphabet 10p coins are in circulation but are all still hard to find. There are lots of known varieties for the Ten Pence, both larger size and current size. See the end of this section and look online for the relevant predecimal.com forum topics. From 2012 onwards the 10p is made of nickel-plated steel and is magnetic.

OBVERSES

OBVERSE 1

(used 1968 - 1984)
D•G•REG•F•D•(date) || ELIZABETH II
Elizabeth II, Dei Gratia Regina, Fidei Defensor
(Elizabeth II, By the Grace of God Queen and Defender of the Faith)
Portrait by: Arnold Machin

OBVERSE 2

(used 1985 - 1992)
ELIZABETH II || D•G•REG•F•D•(date)
Elizabeth II, Dei Gratia Regina, Fidei Defensor
(Elizabeth II, By the Grace of God Queen and Defender of the Faith)
Portrait by: Raphael Maklouf

REVERSES

REVERSE 1 (left)

(used 1968 - 1981)
Lion Passant Guardant
[Part of the crest of England, a lion passant
guardant royally crowned]
10 NEW PENCE
Design by: Christopher Ironside

REVERSE 2 (right)

(used 1982 - 1992)
Lion Passant Guardant
[Part of the crest of England, a lion passant
guardant royally crowned]
10 TEN PENCE
Design by: Christopher Ironside

28.50 mm • 11.31 grammes • cupro-nickel • milled edge

TYPE 1 (obverse 1, reverse 1)

			UNC	As-New	Proof
1968	336,143,250		£0.50	£2.00	
1969	314,008,000		£0.50	£2.00	
1970	133,571,000		£0.50	£2.00	
1971	63,205,000		£0.50	£2.00	£3.00
1972		Proof Only (from sets)	Used: £1.00		£7.00
1973	152,174,000		£0.50	£2.00	£3.00
1974	92,741,000		£0.50	£2.00	£3.00
1975	181,559,000		£0.50	£2.00	£3.00
1976	228,220,000		£0.50	£2.00	£3.00
1977	59,323,000		£0.50	£2.00	£3.00
1978		Proof Only (from sets)	Used: £1.00		£8.00
1979	115,457,000		£0.50	£2.00	£3.00
1980	88,650,000		£0.50	£2.00	£3.00
1981	3,487,000		Used: £1.00	£4.00	£5.00

TYPE 2 (obverse 1, reverse 2)

			UNC	As-New	Proof
1982	205,000 ‡	Used: £2.00	£3.00	£5.00	£6.00
1983	631,000 ‡	Used: £2.00	£3.00	£5.00	£6.00
1984	158,820 ‡	Used: £2.00	£3.00	£5.00	£6.00

TYPE 3 (obverse 2, reverse 2)

			UNC	As-New	Proof
1985	178,000 ‡	Used: £2.00	£3.00	£5.00	£5.00
1986	167,000 ‡	Used: £2.00	£3.00	£5.00	£5.00
1987	172,425 ‡	Used: £2.00	£3.00	£5.00	£5.00
1988	134,067 ‡	Used: £2.00	£3.00	£5.00	£5.00
1989	77,569 ‡	Used: £2.00	£3.00	£5.00	£5.00
1990	102,606 ‡	Used: £2.00	£3.00	£5.00	£5.00
1991	74,975 ‡	Used: £2.00	£3.00	£5.00	£5.00
1992	78,421 ‡	Used: £2.00	£3.00	£5.00	£5.00

NOTES

‡   These years were not issued for circulation, and the "business strikes" were made for BU mint folders, only.

INFO

As of 30th June 1993, the large ten-pence coins were demonetised.

OBVERSES

OBVERSE 3
(used 1992 - 1997)
ELIZABETH II || D•G•REG•F•D•(date)
Elizabeth II, Dei Gratia Regina, Fidei Defensor
(Elizabeth II, By the Grace of God Queen and Defender of the Faith)
Portrait by: Raphael Maklouf

OBVERSE 4
(used 1998 - 2008)
ELIZABETH II•D•G || REG•F•D•(date)
Elizabeth II, Dei Gratia Regina, Fidei Defensor
(Elizabeth II, By the Grace of God Queen and Defender of the Faith)
Portrait by: Ian Rank-Broadley

OBVERSE 5 (similar to last, with no rim beading)
(used 2008 - 2015)
ELIZABETH II•D•G || REG•F•D•(date)
Elizabeth II, Dei Gratia Regina, Fidei Defensor
(Elizabeth II, By the Grace of God Queen and Defender of the Faith)
Portrait by: Ian Rank-Broadley

OBVERSE 6
(used 2015 onwards, except alphabet coins)
ELIZABETH II•DEI•GRA•REG•FID•DEF•(date)
Elizabeth II, Dei Gratia Regina, Fidei Defensor
(Elizabeth II, By the Grace of God Queen and Defender of the Faith)
Portrait by: Jody Clark

REVERSES

REVERSE 3
(used 1992 - 2008)
Lion Passant Guardant
[Part of the crest of England, a lion passant guardant royally crowned]
10 TEN PENCE
Design by: Christopher Ironside

REVERSE 4
(used 2008 to date)
Upper left section of the Royal coat of Arms of the
United Kingdom.
TEN PENCE
Design by: Matthew Dent

TYPE 4 - Reduced in size from 28.5mm to 24.5mm (obverse 3, reverse 3)

			UNC	As-New	Proof
1992	1,413,455,170 [‡1]		£0.30	£3.00	£3.00
1993		Used: £0.50	£2.00	£6.00	£5.00
1994	56,945	In sets only Used: £0.50	£2.00	£4.00	£8.00
1995	43,259,000		£0.30	£3.00	£3.00
1996	118,738,000 [‡2]		£0.30	£3.00	£3.00
1997	99,196,000		£0.30	£3.00	£3.00

TYPE 5 (obverse 4, reverse 3)

			UNC	As-New	Proof
1998	In sets only	(100,000 proofs)	Used: £0.50	£7.00	£6.00
1999	In sets only		Used: £0.50	£7.00	£6.00
2000	134,727,000		£0.30	£2.00	£3.00
2001	82,081,000		£0.30	£2.00	£3.00
2002	80,934,000		£0.30	£2.00	£3.00
2003	88,118,000		£0.30	£2.00	£3.00
2004	99,602,000		£0.30	£3.00	£3.00
2005	69,604,000 [‡1]	'1' of '10' to bead or to space	£0.30	£3.00	£3.00
2006	118,803,000 [‡1]		£0.30	£3.00	£3.00
2007	72,720,000		£0.30	£3.00	£3.00
2008	9,720,000		£0.30	£3.00	£3.00

TYPE 6 (obverse 5, reverse 4. Nickel plated steel from 2012 onwards)

			UNC	As-New	Proof
2008	71,447,000		£0.30	£3.00	£4.00
2009	84,360,000		£0.30	£3.00	£4.00
2009	2 or 3 known*	Mule, rev. 3	£1,000.00		
2010	96,600,500		£0.30	£3.00	£3.00
2011	59,603,850		£0.30	£3.00	£3.00
2012	11,600,030		£0.30	£3.00	£5.00
2013	320,200,750		£0.30	£3.00	£5.00
2014	490,202,020		FV	£4.00	£5.00
2015	119,000,000		FV	£4.00	£5.00

TYPE 7 (obverse 6, reverse 4)

			UNC	As-New	Proof
2015	91,900,000		FV	£4.00	£5.00
2016	135,380,000		FV	£4.00	£5.00
2017	32,300,000		FV	£4.00	£5.00
2018	Not yet known	Currently in sets only		£4.00	£5.00
2019	Not yet known	Currently in sets only		£4.00	£5.00
2020	Not yet known	Currently in sets only		£5.00	

* A mismatch of dies known as a mule has resulted in three (so far) 2009 coins with the incorrect previous reverse (Ironside's "lion passant guardant").

[‡1] Varieties exist for the 1992 issue, see next pages. Variety reverses 1 & 2 have also been noted for 2005 and possibly for 2006 dated coins. It is not yet clear if one type is scarcer than the other.

[‡2] Exists as a silver proof, originally part of a set

The Alphabet Ten Pence coins - 2018 and 2019

Introduced in March 2018, the twenty-six A-Z 10p coins are sold by the Royal Mint, designated as 'early strike' for £2 each. Post offices also sold individual coins for £4 each. They have entered circulation but don't seem to be all that widely distributed and I am not aware of anyone who has actually managed to get all twenty-six from change.

The same alphabet themed coins were also struck again, dated 2019, which means that more should enter circulation and that means that more people will have a chance to collect all the letters. Some completists are less than thrilled though, as it means there are now 52 different 10p coins to collect for 2018 and 2019 (not including the standard shield section reverse). Accurate mintage numbers are not yet known for the 2019 dated coins.

Silver proof versions of the 2018 alphabet 10p's were offered. They appear to cost £35 supplied just in a capsule, or for an extra £10 you even get a box to go with it! I don't think they've been massively popular.

Angel of the North	Bond	Cricket	Double-Decker	English Breakfast
Fish and Chips	Greenwich Meridian	Houses of Parliament	Ice Cream	Jubilee (coach)
King Arthur	Loch Ness Monster	Mackintosh	NHS	Oak
Postbox	Queuing	Robin	Stonehenge	Tea

Union Flag

Village

World Wide Web

X marks the spot

Yeoman Warder

Zebra Crossing

Obverse type - common to all

The slightly higher value coins tend to be the letters that have sold out at the Royal Mint. Many do sell for about the same price in used condition as in As-New condition.

TYPE 8 (obverse 7 with alphabet letter reverse)

2018   Used   As-New
Mintage: 220k for each letter.

2019   Used   As-New
Mintage: 2.1m total for all letters (final figure not yet available).

2018	Used	As-New	2019	Used	As-New
2018 "A"	£4.00	£5.00	2019 "A"	£5.00	£6.00
2018 "B"	£4.00	£5.00	2019 "B"	£4.00	£5.00
2018 "C"	£1.50	£2.00	2019 "C"	£3.00	£4.00
2018 "D"	£1.50	£2.00	2019 "D"	£2.50	£4.00
2018 "E"	£1.50	£2.00	2019 "E"	£2.00	£4.00
2018 "F"	£2.00	£4.00	2019 "F"	£1.50	£4.00
2018 "G"	£2.00	£2.00	2019 "G"	£1.50	£4.00
2018 "H"	£1.50	£2.00	2019 "H"	£1.50	£4.00
2018 "I"	£1.50	£4.00	2019 "I"	£2.00	£4.00
2018 "J"	£1.50	£4.00	2019 "J"	£2.00	£4.00
2018 "K"	£2.00	£2.00	2019 "K"	£2.00	£4.00
2018 "L"	£1.50	£5.00	2019 "L"	£3.00	£4.00
2018 "M"	£1.50	£4.00	2019 "M"	£2.00	£2.00
2018 "N"	£3.00	£6.00	2019 "N"	£3.00	£4.00
2018 "O"	£1.50	£4.00	2019 "O"	£2.00	£2.00
2018 "P"	£2.00	£2.00	2019 "P"	£1.50	£2.00
2018 "Q"	£2.00	£2.00	2019 "Q"	£1.50	£2.00
2018 "R"	£3.00	£4.00	2019 "R"	£3.00	£4.00
2018 "S"	£1.50	£4.00	2019 "S"	£2.00	£2.00
2018 "T"	£2.00	£5.00	2019 "T"	£2.00	£2.00
2018 "U"	£1.50	£2.00	2019 "U"	£1.50	£2.00
2018 "V"	£1.50	£2.00	2019 "V"	£2.00	£4.00
2018 "W"	£1.50	£2.00	2019 "W"	£2.00	£4.00
2018 "X"	£1.50	£2.00	2019 "X"	£1.50	£2.00
2018 "Y"	£2.00	£2.00	2019 "Y"	£2.00	£2.00
2018 "Z"	£2.00	£2.00	2019 "Z"	£3.00	£4.00

TEN PENCE VARIETIES - Early, large size coins

There are a large number of subtle die varieties known for the Ten pence's struck from the earliest in 1968, right through to the 1980s. The varieties first came to light in the 1970s, surveyed (among others) by Ron Stafford, who published a few incredibly detailed articles on them. The majority of the varieties concern the number of beads in the borders and the precise positioning of the letters and digits, in relation to the border beads. It can make your eyes go funny just reading about it!

While significant, I feel that due to the complex nature, space required to list them all and the fact that the varieties are not often differentiated between, that it would perhaps be a better idea to mention them here, but not go in to any detail.

The original information on these early decimal varieties is hard to find, but there are however two highly recommended books on all 20th century coin varieties (including decimals) by David J. Groom entitled 'The Identification of British 20th Century Silver Coin Varieties' and 'The Identification of British 20th Century Bronze Coin Varieties'. Both are available new and can be found online.

TEN PENCE VARIETIES - Later, smaller coins

The production of the new 1992 smaller sized ten pence piece has yielded several varieties, some of which appear to be much less common than others.

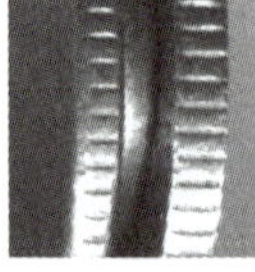

The first type of ten pence pieces have a "wired" edge (left coin in both images), which has a curved edge, while all other varieties have a "flat" sharper edge (right coin in both images).

Obverse 1: The letters L and I in ELIZABETH point between 2 border beads. Obverse 2: The letters L and I in ELIZABETH point directly at border beads.

Reverse 1: The number 1 in the "10" points directly at a border bead. Reverse 2: The number 1 in the "10" points between 2 border beads.

TEN PENCE VARIETIES - Later, smaller coins

1992 Ten Pence types:

TYPE 1: wired edge, obverse 1, reverse 1
Earliest type. It appears that the "wired" edge was abandoned sometime midway through 1992 production. Represents approximately 40% of total mintage.

TYPE 2: flat edge, obverse variety 1, reverse variety 1
A continuation of the TYPE 1, but on different planchets with flat edges. This type also represents approximately 40% of the total mintage.

TYPE 3: flat edge, obverse variety 1, reverse variety 2
An extremely uncommon variety, referred to as the "between/between" type. Represents about 3% of the total mintage, perhaps a little less. This type could become desirable in the future.

TYPE 4: flat edge, obverse variety 2, reverse variety 1
The rarest variety, referred to as the "to dot/to dot" variety. Represents less than 1% of the total mintage, with some estimates as low as one half of 1%. This type may be worth saving for the future.

TYPE 5: flat edge, obverse variety 2, reverse variety 2
This type exhibits a new obverse and reverse style. Represents approximately 15% of the total mintage. This is the type is found in Proof sets and BU Mint folders.
From 1993 to 2006 it seems that the circulation coins all have Reverse 1 (i.e. the '1' of '10' pointing directly at a border bead) and that proof coins and coins in the BU sets have Reverse 2 (the '1' of '10' pointing between two border beads). It is not known 100% if this trend continued up to 2008 (the last year of the old reverse design).

What's currently legal tender?

All 20p coins are legal tender. Victorian Double Florins also appear to be legal tender for 20p (4 shillings) as the author is unable to find any evidence that they were demonetised in 1971 with the rest of the old denominations. To spend one would be quite silly though, as the value of the silver contained within a double florin is far higher than 20p!

Which are hard to find?

The 1986 20p was made to be put in sets only and is therefore incredibly hard to find in change.

The new (2008) design 20p with no date is scarce. This coin is technically known as a mule and occurred because the Royal Mint used the old obverse (OBVERSE 3) die with the new reverse (REVERSE 2) die in error, resulting in a coin with no date on it. All the errors should have been dated 2008 as the error was noticed after apparently between 100,000 to 250,000 coins were struck.

The approximate mintage figure of the mule 20p of 100,000+ would seem to be supported by the quite large volume of these offered for sale. Clearly this is a very low number of coins compared to all of the other 20p annual mintages! But even 100,000 cannot really be deemed as rare. 1,000 would be scarce. 100 would be quite rare. It should be borne in mind though, that rarity alone doesn't always mean high values. High demand and low supply is what causes things to be expensive. This is exactly what happened when the error was made public - all of a sudden thousands of people that wouldn't normally do anything with coins, apart from spend them, all wanted an error 20p and prices were initially very high.

Back to that low mintage number of 100,000 - assuming that low figure is about right, it makes them approximately as scarce as the 1951 British penny. In the 1960s a similar thing happened (a little slower of course, because many people didn't even have televisions and the chap that invented the internet was still in short trousers) and the prices of known scarce coins were artificially inflated by people speculating that they would be a good idea to save for a rainy day. 60-odd years later and an absolutely perfect shimmering BU 1951 penny is worth less than £100 (in real terms, less than what people were paying for them in the 1960s). I could be wrong, but I suspect the same will be true of the mule 20p in 60 years time. They will remain collectable, but the demand will never again outstrip the supply and as a result the values will stay at a more realistic level.

I also predict that in the future the near perfect examples removed from circulation early on will be more sought after than the majority of the coins that were taken from circulation at the point of maximum hype, after being used and abused for 6+ months. The 20p is a popular coin and many that I see for sale are far from perfect even after minimal circulation. Collectors can be fussy and some prefer the very best quality. The mule 20p has so far never been seen in any 2008 year sets.

OBVERSES

OBVERSE 1
(used 1982 - 1984)
ELIZABETH II || D•G•REG•F•D
Elizabeth II, Dei Gratia Regina, Fidei Defensor
(Elizabeth II, By the Grace of God Queen and Defender of the Faith)
Portrait by: Arnold Machin

OBVERSES - continued

OBVERSE 2
(used 1985 - 1997. Altered and made slightly
larger (right image) from 1992 onwards)
ELIZABETH II || D•G•REG•F•D
Elizabeth II, Dei Gratia Regina, Fidei Defensor
(Elizabeth II, By the Grace of God Queen and Defender of the Faith)
Portrait by: Raphael Maklouf

OBVERSE 3
(used 1998 - 2008)
ELIZABETH II || D•G•REG•F•D
Elizabeth II, Dei Gratia Regina, Fidei Defensor
(Elizabeth II, By the Grace of God Queen and Defender of the Faith)
Portrait by: Ian Rank-Broadley

OBVERSE 4
(used 2008 - 2015)
ELIZABETH•II•D•G•REG•F•D•(date)
Elizabeth II, Dei Gratia Regina, Fidei Defensor
(Elizabeth II, By the Grace of God Queen and Defender of the Faith)
Portrait by: Ian Rank-Broadley

OBVERSE 5
(used 2015 onwards)
ELIZABETH II•DEI•GRA•REG•FID•DEF•(date)
Elizabeth II, Dei Gratia Regina, Fidei Defensor
(Elizabeth II, By the Grace of God Queen and Defender of the Faith)
Portrait by: Jody Clark

REVERSES

REVERSE 1
(used 1982 - 2008)
Crowned Tudor Rose
[The Badge of England, a royally crowned double rose]
20 TWENTY PENCE (date)
Design by: William Gardner

REVERSE 2
(used 2008 to date)
Lower right section of the Royal coat of Arms of the
United Kingdom.
TWENTY PENCE
Design by: Matthew Dent

TYPE 1 (obverse 1, reverse 1)

			UNC	As-New	Proof
1982	740,815,000		£0.30	£2.00	£4.00
	Silver piedfort proof				£20.00
1983	158,463,000		£0.50	£3.00	£4.00
1984	65,350,965		£0.50	£3.00	£4.00

TYPE 2 (obverse 2, reverse 1)

			UNC	As-New	Proof
1985	74,273,699		£0.50	£3.00	£4.00
1986	167,000 [2]		£5.00	£10.00	£10.00
1987	137,450,000		£0.50	£3.00	£4.00
1988	38,038,344		£0.50	£3.00	£4.00
1989	132,013,890		£0.50	£3.00	£4.00
1990	88,097,500		£0.50	£3.00	£4.00
1991	35,901,250		£0.50	£3.00	£4.00
1992	31,205,000 (both)	Small head*	£0.50	£3.00	£5.00
1992		Large head*	£1.00	£5.00	exists?
1993	123,123,750		£0.50	£3.00	£4.00
1994	67,131,250		£0.50	£3.00	£4.00
1995	102,005,000		£0.50	£3.00	£4.00
1996	83,163,750	*	£0.50	£3.00	£4.00
1997	89,518,750		£0.50	£3.00	£4.00

TYPE 3 (obverse 3, reverse 1)

		UNC	As-New	Proof
1998	76,965,000	£0.50	£3.00	£4.00
1999	73,478,750	£0.50	£3.00	£4.00
2000	136,418,750	£0.50	£3.00	£4.00
2001	148,122,500	£0.50	£3.00	£4.00
2002	93,360,000	£0.50	£3.00	£4.00
2003	153,383,750	£0.50	£3.00	£4.00
2004	120,212,500	£0.50	£3.00	£4.00
2005	154,488,750	£0.50	£3.00	£4.00
2006	114,800,000	£0.50	£3.00	£4.00
2007	117,075,000	£0.50	£3.00	£4.00
2008	11,900,000	£0.50	£3.00	£5.00

* The 1992 small head coin was thought to be scarcer than the large head, but new information would seem to imply that the large head coins are the coins that were circulated in large numbers and are now hardest to find (especially in top condition as most have seen normal usage). It is now thought that the proof version only exists with the small head. The easiest way to tell the difference is that the small head bust has a much sharper point where the neck ends at the bottom.

1996 also exists as a silver proof, originally part of a set.

21.40 mm • 5.00 grammes • cupro-nickel • plain edge

MULE ERROR (mismatching obverse 3 and reverse 2)

	UNC	As-New	Proof
[2008] Also known as the 'dateless' 20p **Used, up to: £50** £60		£80	-

Chinese made fakes exist. They have a dirty matt appearance, thinner lettering and a lack of detail.

TYPE 4 (obverse 4, reverse 2)

			UNC	As-New	Proof
2008 [3]	115,022,000		FV	£4.00	£5.00
2009	121,625,300		FV	£4.00	£5.00
2010	112,875,500		FV	£4.00	£5.00
2011	191,625,000		FV	£4.00	£5.00
2012	69,650,030		FV	£4.00	£5.00
2013	66,325,000		FV	£4.00	£5.00
2014	173,775,000		FV	£4.00	£5.00
2015	63,175,000		FV	£4.00	£5.00

TYPE 5 (obverse 5 reverse 2)

			UNC	As-New	Proof
2015	131,250,000		FV	£4.00	£5.00
2016	161,000,000		FV	£4.00	£5.00
2017	Not yet known	Currently in sets only		£6.00	£6.00
2018	Not yet known	Currently in sets only		£6.00	£6.00
2019	Not yet known	Currently in sets only		£6.00	£6.00
2020	Not yet known	Currently in sets only		£6.00	

NOTES

[2] Each year, it is determined, based upon supply and demand, what denominations will be struck for circulation. 1986 was not issued for circulation, and the "business strikes" were made for BU mint folders, only.

[3] The 2008 new design (non mule) coin and also some similar 2009 coins exist with what was originally thought to be a small raised '1' on the reverse. It is actually a die crack, rather than any deliberate mint identification mark. Interesting nonetheless, as a few of these are known to exist. This same '1' die crack coin has also been reported dated 2010, but is yet to be confirmed.

2008 20p reverse with small '1'.

Historically the Crown was five shillings (one quarter of a 20 shilling pound). For that reason, the new decimal crowns initially had a face value of 25p. These four commemorative crown coins are legal tender for 25p, but they are rarely used by the public, probably because they are too big to be convenient, and to collectors they are usually worth a little more than face value. Members of the public often assume incorrectly that these four coins have a face value of £5. The crown was re-valued as £5 in 1990, although the size and weight of the coin remained the same.

For later Crowns, see the FIVE POUNDS sections.

These four coins were issued to mark the following occasions: 1972 — The 25th Wedding Anniversary of the Queen and Prince Philip. 1977 - The Silver Jubilee of the Queen. 1980 - The 80th Birthday of the Queen Mother. 1981 - The Royal Wedding of Charles and Diana.

COMMEMORATIVE TYPE 1
Obverse: Standard portrait of QE II
Design by: Arnold Machin

Reverse: Elizabeth and Philip,
20 November 1947-1972
Design by: Arnold Machin

			As-New	Proof
1972	7,452,100		£1.50	£4.00
	100,000	.925 sterling silver proof		£20.00

COMMEMORATIVE TYPE 2
Obverse: Equestrian portrait of QE II
Design by: Arnold Machin

Reverse: Ampulla and anointing spoon, items used during the Coronation
Design by: Arnold Machin

		As-New	Proof
1977	37,061,160	£1.00	£4.00
Specimen in folder		£1.00	
377,000	.925 sterling silver proof		£15.00

COMMEMORATIVE TYPE 3
Obverse: Standard portrait of QE II
Design by: Arnold Machin

Reverse: Portrait of Queen Mother, surrounded by bows and lions
Design by: Richard Guyatt

		As-New	Proof
1980	9,306,000	£1.50	-
Specimen in folder		£2.00	
83,672	.925 sterling silver proof		£20.00

COMMEMORATIVE TYPE 4
Obverse: Standard portrait of QE II
Design by: Arnold Machin

Reverse: Conjoined busts of Charles & Diana
Design by: Philip Nathan

		As-New	Proof
1981	26,773,600	£1.50	-
Specimen in folder		£2.00	
218,000	.925 sterling silver proof		£20.00
Set of 4 (72, 77, 80 and 81) Crowns as silver proofs in large case. 5,000 sets issued			£65.00

33

What's currently legal tender?

Only the smaller (post-1997) 50p coins are legal tender now. Most banks will allow you to pay in the pre-1997 larger 30mm coins.

Which are hard to find?

The most valuable 50p that could potentially be found in change is the withdrawn Olympic Aquatics coin with the lines on the swimmers' face. See Commemorative Type 17. The prices for the Kew Gardens 2009 50p remain high, following media exposure when it was established a few years later that this particular coin has the lowest mintage of all the circulating 50p coins. The 1992-1993 EU coin is also higher priced after it was hyped up as being the older larger-size 50p with the lowest mintage. 2009 dated Blue Peter high jump 50p coins are also in demand.

Special proof sets of 50p coins were made in 2009 and proof/BU sets were made in 2019. All of the coins are the newer 27.3mm size and all feature the portrait of the Queen current in 2009 and 2019 respectively. See info after commemorative type 5 for the 2009 set and info after commemorative type 69 for the 2019 sets.

OBVERSES

OBVERSE 1

(used 1969 - 1972, 1974 - 1984)
D•G•REG•F•D•(date) || ELIZABETH II
Elizabeth II, Dei Gratia Regina, Fidei Defensor
(Elizabeth II, By the Grace of God Queen and Defender of the Faith)
Portrait by: Arnold Machin

OBVERSE 2

(used 1985 - 1997)
ELIZABETH II || D•G•REG•F•D•(date)
Elizabeth II, Dei Gratia Regina, Fidei Defensor
(Elizabeth II, By the Grace of God Queen and Defender of the Faith)
Portrait by: Raphael Maklouf

REVERSES

REVERSE 1 (left)

(used 1969 - 1972, 1974 - 1981 and for 2019 commemoratives)
Britannia
[The seated figure of Britannia]
50 NEW PENCE
Design by: Christopher Ironside

REVERSE 2 (right)

(used 1982 - 93, 1995 - 1997)
Britannia
[The seated figure of Britannia]
50 FIFTY PENCE
Design by: Christopher Ironside

30 mm • 13.5 grammes • cupro-nickel • plain edge

DEFINITIVE TYPE 1 (obverse 1, reverse 1)

			UNC	As-New	Proof
1969	188,400,000		£1.00	£2.00	
1970	19,461,500	Used: £4.00	£6.00	£10.00	
1971		Proof Only (from the sets)	Used: £1.00		£5.00
1972		Proof Only (from the sets)	Used: £1.00		£5.00
1974		Proof Only (from the sets)	Used: £1.00		£5.00
1975		Proof Only (from the sets)	Used: £1.00		£5.00
1976	43,746,500		£1.00	£3.00	£4.00
1977	49,536,000		£1.00	£3.00	£4.00
1978	72,005,500		£1.00	£3.00	£4.00
1979	58,680,000		£1.00	£3.00	£4.00
1980	89,086,000		£1.00	£3.00	£4.00
1981	74,002,000		£1.00	£3.00	£4.00

DEFINITIVE TYPE 2 (obverse 1, reverse 2)

			UNC	As-New	Proof
1982	51,312,000		£1.00	£3.00	£4.00
1983	62,824,904		£1.00	£3.00	£4.00
1984	158,820 ‡	Used: £2.00	£3.00	£8.00	£8.00

DEFINITIVE TYPE 3 (obverse 2, reverse 2)

			UNC	As-New	Proof
1985	682,103	Used: £5.00	£7.00	£10.00	£8.00
1986	167,000 ‡	Used: £4.00	£5.00	£8.00	£8.00
1987	172,425 ‡	Used: £4.00	£5.00	£8.00	£8.00
1988	134,067 ‡	Used: £4.00	£5.00	£8.00	£8.00
1989	77,569 ‡	Used: £4.00	£5.00	£8.00	£8.00
1990	102,606 ‡	Used: £4.00	£5.00	£8.00	£8.00
1991	74,975 ‡	Used: £4.00	£5.00	£8.00	£8.00
1992	78,421 ‡	Used: £4.00	£5.00	£8.00	£8.00
1993	56,945 ‡	Used: £4.00	£5.00	£8.00	£8.00
1994	Smaller type. Marked 'ROYAL MINT TRIAL'	Used: £1,200.00 (see below)			
1995	105,647 ‡	Used: £4.00	£5.00	£8.00	£8.00
1996	86,501 ‡	Used: £4.00	£5.00	£8.00	£8.00
1997	‡	Used: £1.00	£3.00	£8.00	£8.00

‡   These years were not issued for circulation, and the "business strikes" were made for BU mint folders, only.

Below: Rare 1994 50p trial coins, one round, one conventionally shaped.

COLLECTORS' COINS - DECIMAL ISSUES OF THE UK

OBVERSES

OBVERSE 3
(used 1997)
ELIZABETH II || D•G•REG•F•D•(date)
Elizabeth II, Dei Gratia Regina, Fidei Defensor
(Elizabeth II, By the Grace of God Queen and Defender of the Faith)
Portrait by: Raphael Maklouf

OBVERSE 4
(used 1998 - 2008 and for most commemorative coins
1998 - 2015, except where shown)
ELIZABETH II || D•G•REG•F•D•(date)
Elizabeth II, Dei Gratia Regina, Fidei Defensor
(Elizabeth II, By the Grace of God Queen and Defender of the Faith)
Portrait by: Ian Rank-Broadley

OBVERSE 5 (similar to last, with different alignment)
(used 2008 - 2015, with Reverse 4)
ELIZABETH II || D•G•REG•F•D•(date)
Elizabeth II, Dei Gratia Regina, Fidei Defensor
(Elizabeth II, By the Grace of God Queen and Defender of the Faith)
Portrait by: Ian Rank-Broadley

OBVERSE 6
(used 2015 onwards, with variations for commemorative coins)
ELIZABETH II•DEI•GRA•REG•FID•DEF•(date)
Elizabeth II, Dei Gratia Regina, Fidei Defensor
(Elizabeth II, By the Grace of God Queen and Defender of the Faith)
Portrait by: Jody Clark

REVERSES

REVERSE 3
(used 1997 - 2008)
Often referred to as the 'Britannia issue' to distinguish it from the
commemorative issues.
[The seated figure of Britannia]
50 FIFTY PENCE
Design by: Christopher Ironside

REVERSE 4
(used 2008 to date)
Bottom section of the Royal coat of Arms of the
United Kingdom.
FIFTY PENCE
Design by: Matthew Dent

DEFINITIVE TYPE 4 - Reduced size from 30mm to 27.3mm (obverse 3, reverse 3)

			UNC	As-New	Proof
1997	456,364,100		£2.00	£5.00	£5.00

DEFINITIVE TYPE 5 (obverse 4, reverse 3)

			UNC	As-New	Proof
1998	64,306,500		£2.00	£5.00	
1999	24,905,000		£2.00	£5.00	£5.00
2000	27,915,500		£2.00	£5.00	£5.00
2001	84,998,500		£2.00	£5.00	£5.00
2002	23,907,500		£2.00	£5.00	£5.00
2003	23,583,000		£2.00	£5.00	£5.00
2004	35,315,500		£2.00	£5.00	£5.00
2005	25,363,500		£2.00	£5.00	£5.00
2006	24,567,000	(not in BU sets)	£5.00		£5.00
2007	11,200,000	(not in BU sets)	£5.00		£5.00
2008	3,500,000	Used: £1.00	£4.00	£6.00	£7.00

DEFINITIVE TYPE 6 (obverse 5, reverse 4)

			UNC	As-New	Proof
2008	22,747,000		£2.00	£5.00	£3.00
2009	None for circulation*	(108,816 in BU sets) up to	£50.00		no data
2010	None for circulation*	(69,189 in BU sets) up to	£28.00		no data
2011	None for circulation*	(56,007 in BU sets) up to	£50.00		no data
2012	32,300,030		£2.00	£5.00	£5.00
2013	10,301,000		£2.00	£5.00	£5.00
2014	49,001,000		£2.00	£5.00	£6.00
2015	20,101,000		£2.00	£6.00	£6.00

* Currently these seem to have a value in used condition of around £20 for the 2010 and £35
each for the 2009 and 2011 coins. They are very rarely found in change.

DEFINITIVE TYPE 7 (obverse 6, reverse 4)

			UNC	As-New	Proof
2015	39,300,000			£6.00	£6.00
2016	None for circulation (38,502 in BU sets)	Used: £10		£40.00	no data
2017	1,800,000	Used: £1.50		£6.00	£6.00
2018	Not yet known	Currently in sets only		£5.00	£5.00
2019	Not yet known	(seen in circulation)		£5.00	£5.00
2020	Not yet known	Currently in sets only		£5.00	£5.00

37

COMMEMORATIVE TYPE 1

1973 || 50 || pence (centre)
Nine clasped hands forming a circle
(Britain's entry into the European
Economic Community)
Reverse design by: David Wynne
(also exists dated 2009, see page 39)

		Used	As-New	Proof
1973	89,775,000	£1.00	£3.00	£3.00
	Proof in leatherette case			£4.00
	Thick planchet but not recorded as Piedfort			Extremely Rare

COMMEMORATIVE TYPE 2

1992-1993 (upper) || 50 pence (lower)
Conference table with seats and stars
(completion of the EC single market and
the British Presidency)
Reverse design by: Mary Milner Dickens
(also exists dated 2009, see page 39)

		Used	UNC/As-New	Proof
1992-1993	109,000	£50.00*	£70.00	£0.00
	Specimen in folder (including Britannia issue)		£80.00	
	26,890	.925 sterling silver proof		£60.00
	15,000	.925 sterling silver piedfort proof		£80.00
	1,864	.917 gold proof		£900.00

*Since being reported as the old size 50p with the lowest mintage, interest and prices have increased. Used examples aren't encountered that often.

COMMEMORATIVE TYPE 3

50 pence (lower right)
Ships and planes taking part in the
D-Day landings
(50th Anniversary of the D-Day Invasion)
Reverse design by: John Mills
(also exists dated 2009 and 2019,
see pages 39 and 66)

		Used	As-New	Proof
1994	6,705,520	£3.00	£4.00	£8.00
	Specimen in folder		£7.00	
	40,500	.925 sterling silver proof		£25.00
	10,000	.925 sterling silver piedfort proof		£35.00
	1,877	.917 gold proof		£900.00

COMMEMORATIVE TYPE 4

1973 EU 1998 || 50 pence (lower)
Fireworks pattern of 12 stars
(25th Anniversary - UK entry into EEC)
Design by: John Mills
(also exists dated 2009, see below)

		Used	As-New	Proof
1998	5,043,000	£1.00	£4.00	£8.00
15,370	Specimen in folder (including Britannia issue)		£18.00	
8,854	.925 sterling silver proof			£25.00
5,117	.925 sterling silver piedfort proof			£40.00
1,177	.917 gold proof			£600.00

COMMEMORATIVE TYPE 5

FIFTIETH ANNIVERSARY (upper) || 50 pence (lower)
Caring Hands, holding sun's rays
(50th Anniversary - National Health Service)
Design by: Mary Milner Dickens
(also exists dated 2009, see below)

		Used	As-New	Proof
1998	5,001,000	£1.00	£4.00	
	Specimen in folder		£14.00	
9,029	.925 sterling silver proof			£20.00
5,117	.925 sterling silver piedfort proof			£25.00
651	.917 gold proof			£600.00

The 2009 retrospective 40th Anniversary set of sixteen fifty pence coins.

From the introduction of the 50p in 1969 up to and including the 2009 Kew Gardens coin there were a total of 16 different 50p reverses used. These large types:

Standard Britannia with 'NEW PENCE' (REVERSE 1)
EEC Hands (commemorative TYPE 1)
Standard Britannia with 'FIFTY PENCE' (REVERSE 2)
EC 1992-1993 (commemorative TYPE 2)
D-Day (commemorative TYPE 3)

And also the smaller commemorative types 4 to 13 and the REVERSE 4 of the normal 50p.

All of these designs were sold in sets of 16, all featuring OBVERSE 4 and all being of the newer 27.3mm diameter, even the five listed above that were originally larger. Just over 1000 of each cupro-nickel or silver sets were made and they are both hard to find. Value: £600 - £700.

Very rare: There were also 70 gold proof sets and 40 gold proof piedfort sets sold!

39

27.3 mm • 8.0 grammes • cupro-nickel • plain edge

COMMEMORATIVE TYPE 6
1850-2000 (upper) || PUBLIC LIBRARIES (lower)
Open book upon pillared building
(150th Anniversary - British Libraries)
Design by: Mary Milner Dickens
(also exists dated 2009, see page 39)

			As-New	Proof
2000	11,263,000		£4.00	£8.00
		Specimen in folder	£14.00	
		.925 sterling silver proof		£25.00
	5,721	.925 sterling silver piedfort proof		£30.00
	710	.917 gold proof		£550.00

COMMEMORATIVE TYPE 7
50 pence (left) || 1903-2003 (lower right)
Suffragette with WSPU banner
(100th Anniversary - Women's Social and Political Union)
Design by: Mary Milner Dickens
(also exists dated 2009, see page 39)

			Used	As-New	Proof
2003	3,124,030	(43,513 proofs in sets)	£2.00	£16.00	£12.00
	9,582	Specimen in folder		£30.00	
	6,267 of 15k	.925 sterling silver proof			£25.00
	6,795 of 7.5k	.925 sterling silver piedfort proof			£40.00
	942 of 1000	.917 gold proof			£550.00

* Increased value recently due to someone 'discovering' 13 years later that 3.1m mintage is on the low side compared to most other 50p coins!

COMMEMORATIVE TYPE 8
50 pence (lower)
Runner's legs and stopwatch
(50th Anniversary - Roger Bannister's 4-minute mile run)
Design by: James Butler
(also exists dated 2009 and 2019, see pages 39 and 63)

			As-New	Proof
2004	9,032,500	(35,020 proofs in sets)	£4.00	£8.00
	10,371	Specimen in folder	£15.00	
	4,924 of 15k	.925 sterling silver proof		£20.00
	4,054 of 7.5k	.925 sterling silver piedfort proof		£35.00
	644 of 1,250	.917 gold proof		£550.00

COMMEMORATIVE TYPE 9
50 (upper) || JOHNSON'S DICTIONARY 1755 (lower)
Dictionary entries for Fifty and Pence
(250th Anniversary - Samuel Johnson's English Dictionary)
Design by: Tom Phillips
(also exists dated 2009, see page 39)

			As-New	Proof
2005	17,649,000	(40,563 proofs in sets)	£4.00	£8.00
	4,029 of 7,50	.925 sterling silver proof		£25.00
	3,808 of 5,000	.925 sterling silver piedfort proof		£30.00
	1,000	.917 gold proof		£550.00

Also, 10,822 BU coins sold in packs with the 2005 £2 (Gunpowder plot) and 2005 £1 (Menai bridge). Value: £20

COMMEMORATIVE TYPE 10
FIFTY PENCE (lower)
Representation of the heroic acts performed by VC recipients
(150th Anniversary - Institution of the Victoria Cross)
Design by: Clive Duncan
(also exists dated 2009 and 2019, see pages 39 and 66)

			As-New	Proof
2006	10,000,500*	(37,689 proofs in sets)	£4.00	£8.00
	37,176	Specimen in folder	£6.00	
	6,872 of 7,500	.925 sterling silver proof		£30.00
	3,415 of 5,000	.925 sterling silver piedfort proof		£40.00
	804 of 1000	.917 gold proof		£550.00

COMMEMORATIVE TYPE 11
VC || FIFTY PENCE
The obverse and reverse of the Victoria Cross
(150th Anniversary - Institution of the Victoria Cross)
Design by: Claire Aldridge
(also exists dated 2009 and 2019, see pages 39 and 66)

			As-New	Proof
2006	12,087,000*	(37,689 proofs in sets)	£4.00	£8.00
	37,176	Specimen in folder	£6.00	
	6,310 of 7,500	.925 sterling silver proof		£30.00
	3,532 of 5,000	.925 sterling silver piedfort proof		£30.00
	866 of 1000	.917 gold proof		£550.00

* Pair of Type 10 and Type 11 coins in folder: £9.00

27.3 mm • 8.0 grammes • cupro-nickel • plain edge

COMMEMORATIVE TYPE 12

FIFTY PENCE | 1907 | BE PREPARED | 2007
The scouting badge
(100th Anniversary - The Scout Movement)
Design by: Kerry Jones
(also exists dated 2009 and 2019, see pages 39 and 63)

			UNC	As-New	Proof
2007	7,710,750	(38,215 proofs in sets)	£1.00	£4.00	£6.00
	28,942	Specimen in folder		£20.00	
	10,895 of 12,500	.925 sterling silver proof			£30.00
	1,555 of 5,000	.925 sterling silver piedfort proof			£35.00
	1,250	.917 gold proof			£550.00

COMMEMORATIVE TYPE 13

1759 2009 | KEW
Chinese Pagoda
(250th Anniversary - Kew Gardens)
Design by: Christopher Le Brun
(also exists dated 2019, see page 63)

			Used	UNC/As-New	Proof
2009	210,000	(34,438 proofs in sets)	£115.00	£130/£160	£160.00
	11,281	Specimen in folder		£250.00	
	7,575	.925 sterling silver proof			£350.00
	2,967	.925 sterling silver piedfort proof			£400.00
	629 of 1,000	.917 gold proof			£1,500-£2,000

Beware of recent Chinese made Kew Gardens 50p fakes. Some are marked as 'COPY' but many are not! The quality of the Queen's portrait tends to be poor, especially around the eye.

The Kew Gardens 50p remains the most expensive circulation type 50p and is still very much in demand. Many that use the Royal Mint 'Coin Hunt' folders simply cannot bear the thought of having a gap in their folder and finding one in change these days is a rare occurrence. There are speculators involved too, and prices fluctuate a little over time. Odd how there was absolutely no demand for them and they could be purchased for a couple of pounds before the mintage number was published - I still believe that far too much emphasis is put on mintage numbers these days.

A total of 210,000 (it's actually over 400k if the single packaged coins and those in the BU year-sets are included) is pretty low compared the other fifty-pences that are currently in circulation, but there are theoretically plenty to go round, as there simply aren't anywhere near 400k people in the world that really want one to keep, and not just to turn a profit on.

COMMEMORATIVE TYPE 14
50 PENCE
An Olympic High Jumper - Obverse dated 2009
(The young viewers of Blue Peter were invited to submit
entries for the design - This was the winner)
Design by: Florence Jackson (aged 9)
Obverse: 4

As-New

2009	Initially 100k were planned, it appears to have been reduced to a max. limit of 50k. Only 19,722 were sold.		
	Specimen on card only (this coin was not circulated) **Used:no data**		£200.00

The mintage number of this coin wasn't made available until fairly recently. Gradually people are realising that very few were sold and even though they were just a few pounds a few years ago, more people want one now. The increased demand has driven the value up and continues to do so.

COMMEMORATIVE TYPE 15
CELEBRATING ONE HUNDRED YEARS OF GIRLGUIDING UK | 50 | PENCE
Girl Guide emblems
(100th Anniversary - The Girl Guides)
Design by: Jonathan Evans and Donna Hainan
(also exists dated 2019, see page 63)

			As-New	Proof
2010	7,410,090		£4.00	£10.00
	36,693	Specimen in folder	£10.00	
	5,271	.925 sterling silver proof		£35.00
	2,879	.925 sterling silver piedfort proof		£50.00
	355	.917 gold proof		no data

COMMEMORATIVE TYPE 16
WWF / 2011
Animal and plant shapes
(50th Anniversary - Word Wildlife Fund)
Design by: Matthew Dent

		Used	As-New	Proof
2011	3,400,000	£1.00	£10.00	£12.00
	11,983	Specimen in folder	£35.00	
	24,870	.925 sterling silver proof		£45.00
	2,244	.925 sterling silver piedfort proof		£100.00
	243 of 1,000	.917 gold proof		no data

* Increased value recently due to someone 'discovering' five years later that 3.4m mintage is on the low side compared to most other 50p coins. They should only be worth 50p in used condition!

27.3 mm • 8.0 grammes • cupro-nickel • plain edge

COMMEMORATIVE TYPE 17 (Olympic 1)
50 PENCE
Swimmer
(London 2012 Olympics - Aquatics)
Design by: Jonathan Olliffe
Obverse: 4

		Used	As-New
2011	2,179,000	£1.50	£16.00
157,990	Specimen sealed on card		£16.00
	Withdrawn coin. Error - lines on face etc, right image £1,100.00*		

* Manipulated normal coins with extra scratched lines on the face exist. Chinese made fakes are also plentiful (sometimes even in fake packaging) and continue to plague eBay and other online selling platforms.

COMMEMORATIVE TYPE 18 (Olympic 2)
50 PENCE
Hand Pulling an Arrow
(London 2012 Olympics - Archery)
Design by: Piotr Powaga
Obverse: 4

		Used	As-New
2011	3,345,500	£1.50	£7.00
140,195	Specimen sealed on card		£8.00

COMMEMORATIVE TYPE 19 (Olympic 3)
50 PENCE
An Olympic High jumper - Obverse dated 2011
(London 2012 Olympics - Athletics, see also Commemorative type 14)
Design by: Florence Jackson (aged 9)
Obverse: 4

		Used	As-New
2011	2,224,000	£1.50	£7.00
168,498	Specimen sealed on card		£8.00

COMMEMORATIVE TYPE 20 (Olympic 4)
50 PENCE
Shuttlecock
(London 2012 Olympics - Badminton)
Design by: Emma Kelly
Obverse: 4

		Used	As-New
2011	2,133,500	£1.50	£7.00
124,237	Specimen sealed on card		£8.00

COMMEMORATIVE TYPE 21 (Olympic 5)
50 PENCE
Players on Ball-Textured Background
(London 2012 Olympics - Basketball)
Design by: Sarah Payne
Obverse: 4

		Used	As-New
2011	1,748,000	£2.00	£7.00
137,157	Specimen sealed on card in undamaged plastic		£30.00
	.925 Silver BU - See note, page 53		£20.00

COMMEMORATIVE TYPE 22 (Olympic 6)
50 PENCE
Player
(London 2012 Olympics - Boccia)
Design by: Justin Chung
Obverse: 4

		Used	As-New
2011	2,166,000	£1.50	£7.00
126,662	Specimen sealed on card		£8.00

45

27.3 mm • 8.0 grammes • cupro-nickel • plain edge

COMMEMORATIVE TYPE 23 (Olympic 7)
50 PENCE
Boxing Gloves with Ring Ropes
(London 2012 Olympics - Boxing)
Design by: Shane Abery
Obverse: 4

		Used	As-New
2011	2,148,500	£1.50	£7.00
142,151	Specimen sealed on card		£8.00

COMMEMORATIVE TYPE 24 (Olympic 8)
50 PENCE
Canoeist in Choppy Waters
(London 2012 Olympics - Canoeing)
Design by: Timothy Lees
Obverse: 4

		Used	As-New
2011	2,166,500	£1.50	£7.00
116,114	Specimen sealed on card		£8.00

COMMEMORATIVE TYPE 25 (Olympic 9)
50 PENCE
Cyclist
(London 2012 Olympics - Cycling)
Design by: Theo Crutchley-Mack
Obverse: 4

		Used	As-New
2011	2,090,500	£1.50	£7.00
156,872	Specimen sealed on card		£8.00
	.925 Silver Proof - See note, page 53		£20.00

COMMEMORATIVE TYPE 26 (Olympic 10)
50 PENCE
Horse, Jumping
(London 2012 Olympics - Equestrian)
Design by: Thomas Babbage
Obverse: 4

		Used	As-New
2011	2,142,500	£1.50	£7.00
145,122	Specimen sealed on card		£9.00

COMMEMORATIVE TYPE 27 (Olympic 11)
50 PENCE
Fencing
(London 2012 Olympics - Fencing)
Design by: Ruth Summerfield
Obverse: 4

		Used	As-New
2011	2,115,500	£1.50	£7.00
130,815	Specimen sealed on card		£9.00

COMMEMORATIVE TYPE 28 (Olympic 12)
OFFSIDE EXPLAINED / 50 PENCE
Diagram of the Offside Rule
(London 2012 Olympics - Football)
Design by: Neil Wolfson
Obverse: 4

		Used	As-New
2011	1,125,500	£12.00	£25.00
188,262	Specimen sealed on card		£25.00

27.3 mm • 8.0 grammes • cupro-nickel • plain edge

COMMEMORATIVE TYPE 29 (Olympic 13)
50 PENCE
Player with Ball
(London 2012 Olympics - Goalball)
Design by: Jonathan Wren
Obverse: 4

		Used	As-New
2011	1,615,500	£2.50	£7.00
114,334	Specimen sealed on card		£9.00

COMMEMORATIVE TYPE 30 (Olympic 14)
50 PENCE
Gymnast
(London 2012 Olympics - Gymnastics)
Design by: Jonathan Olliffe
Obverse: 4

		Used	As-New
2011	1,720,813	£2.00	£7.00
145,895	Specimen sealed on card		£9.00

COMMEMORATIVE TYPE 31 (Olympic 15)
50 PENCE
Player with Ball
(London 2012 Olympics - Handball)
Design by: Natasha Ratcliffe
Obverse: 4

		Used	As-New
2011	1,676,500	£1.50	£7.00
117,566	Specimen sealed on card		£9.00

COMMEMORATIVE TYPE 32 (Olympic 16)
50 PENCE
Two Hockey Players
(London 2012 Olympics - Hockey)
Design by: Robert Evans
Obverse: 4

		Used	As-New
2011	1,773,500	£2.50	£7.00
130,813	Specimen sealed on card		£9.00

COMMEMORATIVE TYPE 33 (Olympic 17)
50 PENCE
Judo Throw
(London 2012 Olympics - Judo)
Design by: David Cornell
Obverse: 4

		Used	As-New
2011	1,161,500	£8.50	£17.00
128,442	Specimen sealed on card		£20.00

COMMEMORATIVE TYPE 34 (Olympic 18)
50 PENCE
Swimmer and four Silhouettes
(London 2012 Olympics - Modern Pentathlon)
Design by: Daniel Brittain
Obverse: 4

		Used	As-New
2011	1,689,500	£2.00	£7.00
123,357	Specimen sealed on card		£9.00

27.3 mm • 8.0 grammes • cupro-nickel • plain edge

COMMEMORATIVE TYPE 35 (Olympic 19)
50 PENCE
Slogans and Two Rowers
(London 2012 Olympics - Rowing)
Design by: Davey Podmore
Obverse: 4

		Used	As-New
2011	1,717,300	£2.00	£7.00
140,997	Specimen sealed on card		£9.00

COMMEMORATIVE TYPE 36 (Olympic 20)
50 PENCE
Sailing Boats on the Sea
(London 2012 Olympics - Sailing)
Design by: Bruce Rushin
Obverse: 4

		Used	As-New
2011	1,749,500	£2.00	£7.00
138,535	Specimen sealed on card		£9.00

COMMEMORATIVE TYPE 37 (Olympic 21)
50 PENCE
Figure, Shooting
(London 2012 Olympics - Shooting)
Design by: Pravin Dewdhory
Obverse: 4

		Used	As-New
2011	1,656,500	£2.50	£7.00
125,398	Specimen sealed on card		£9.00

COMMEMORATIVE TYPE 38 (Olympic 22)
50 PENCE
Table Tennis Bats, Ball etc
(London 2012 Olympics - Table Tennis)
Design by: Alan Linsdell
Obverse: 4

		Used	As-New
2011	1,737,500	£2.00	£7.00
123,195	Specimen sealed on card		£9.00

COMMEMORATIVE TYPE 39 (Olympic 23)
50 PENCE
Two Figures Participating in Taekwando
(London 2012 Olympics - Taekwando)
Design by: David Gibbons
Obverse: 4

		Used	As-New
2011	1,664,000	£2.00	£7.00
120,210	Specimen sealed on card		£9.00

COMMEMORATIVE TYPE 40 (Olympic 24)
50 PENCE
Tennis Ball and Net
(London 2012 Olympics - Tennis)
Design by: Tracy Baines
Obverse: 4

		Used	As-New	Proof
2011	1,454,000	£3.00	£7.00	
144,535	Specimen sealed on card		£9.00	

27.3 mm • 8.0 grammes • cupro-nickel • plain edge

COMMEMORATIVE TYPE 41 (Olympic 25)
50 PENCE
Silhouettes of Runner, Cyclist and Swimmer
(London 2012 Olympics - Triathlon)
Design by: Sarah Harvey
Obverse: 4

		Used	As-New
2011	1,163,500	£9.00	£16.00
146,354	Specimen sealed on card		£20.00

COMMEMORATIVE TYPE 42 (Olympic 26)
50 PENCE
Three Players and Central Net
(London 2012 Olympics - Volleyball)
Design by: Daniela Boothman
Obverse: 4

		Used	As-New
2011	2,133,500	£1.50	£7.00
124,115	Specimen sealed on card		£9.00

COMMEMORATIVE TYPE 43 (Olympic 27)
50 PENCE
Basic Outline of a Weightlifter
(London 2012 Olympics - Weightlifting)
Design by: Rob Shakespeare
Obverse: 4

		Used	As-New
2011	1,879,500	£1.50	£7.00
121,778	Specimen sealed on card		£10.00

COMMEMORATIVE TYPE 44 (Olympic 28)

50 PENCE

Man Playing, Ball in Lap
(London 2012 Olympics - Wheelchair Rugby)
Design by: Natasha Ratcliffe
Obverse: 4

		Used	As-New
2011	1,765,500	£2.00	£7.00
121,175	Specimen sealed on card		£10.00
	.925 Silver BU - See note, below		£20.00

COMMEMORATIVE TYPE 45 (Olympic 29)

50 PENCE

Wrestlers
(London 2012 Olympics - Wrestling)
Design by: Roderick Enriquez
Obverse: 4

		Used	As-New
2011	1,129,500	£7.00	£12.00
127,279	Specimen sealed on card		£15.00

Olympic 30

Medallion Only (309,013 were sold.)
The Royal Mint issued a medallion with the 29x 50p coins. It's not
a coin, but is mentioned here for completeness. Values are around
£30 - £40.
Similar 'completer' medals were issued later with a different non
Olympic design and are usually cheaper.

The 50p Olympic Coins - Silver BU versions

All of the olympic 50p coins were also sold in silver BU form. They tend to sell for £25-£35 each.

Gold Versions: Gold proofs were struck by the Royal Mint and just given to the designers of the
coins. They are therefore extremely rare!

27.3 mm • 8.0 grammes • cupro-nickel • plain edge

COMMEMORATIVE TYPE 46
FIFTY PENCE / 50
Ironside's rejected design for the original 1969 50p
(This is what the original Britannia 50p could have looked like)
Design by: Christopher Ironside
Obverse: 4

		Used	As-New	Proof
2013	7,000,000	£1.00	£30.00	£27.00
4,403	Specimen in folder		£100.00	
1,823 of 4.5k	.925 sterling silver proof			£50.00
816 of 1,500	.925 sterling silver piedfort proof			£90.00
198 of 340	.917 gold proof, price new			£800.00

COMMEMORATIVE TYPE 47
BENJAMIN / COMPOSER BORN 1913 / BRITTEN
His name in a double stave, 'Blow Bugle blow' and 'Set the wild echoes flying'.
(To mark the centenary of the birth of Benjamin Britten)
Design by: Tom Phillips

		Used	As-New	Proof
2013	5,300,000	£1.00	£35.00	
5,098	Specimen in folder		£60.00	
717 of 2k	.925 sterling silver proof*			£150.00
515 of 1000	.925 sterling silver piedfort proof			£200.00
70 of 150	.917 gold proof, price new			£1,000.00

*The relatively low silver proof mintage combined with some tabloid hype caused this one to rise in value during 2016. People were also asking silly prices for the normal circulation coin as a result!

COMMEMORATIVE TYPE 48
XX / COMMONWEALTH GAMES GLASGOW / 2014
Male cyclist and female runner
(To commemorate the 20th Commonwealth Games)
Design by: Alex Loudon and Dan Flashman

		UNC	As-New	Proof
2014	6,500,000	£1.00	£4.00	£12.00
14,581*	Specimen in folder		£12.00	
2159 of 2.5k	.925 sterling silver proof			£45.00
992 of 1000	.925 sterling silver piedfort proof			£80.00
233 of 260	.917 gold proof, price new			£725.00

*plus 7,918 sold with stamps.

COMMEMORATIVE TYPE 49a
THE BATTLE OF BRITAIN 1940
<u>**WITHOUT DENOMINATION**</u>
(Pilots scrambling, planes in flight above)
Design by: Gary Breeze & Lee Breeze
Obverse: 4
(Ian Rank-Broadley portrait, as shown)

Note that the denomination is omitted on all coins with the Ian Rank-Broadley portrait (from the 2015 sets), shown here. Apparently deliberate, but I'm sure this was actually an oversight! Confusingly, silver proof and silver piedfort proofs also exist, originally only as part of sets made early in 2015.

		Used	As-New	Proof
2015	(4th portrait, originally in sets only)	£5.00	£14.00	£30.00
35,199	Specimen in folder		£20.00	
1500 max	.925 sterling silver proof, only available in sets of 5x 2015 coins			£75.00?
1500 max	.925 sterling silver piedfort proof, only available in sets as above			£100.00?

COMMEMORATIVE TYPE 49b
THE BATTLE OF BRITAIN 1940
<u>**ALSO WITHOUT DENOMINATION**</u>
Precious metal proofs only, reverse as 49a
(Jody Clark portrait, no denomination, as shown)

Bizarrely the main issue precious metal proof coins have the new portrait, but are also missing the denomination.

		Proof
2015	(5th portrait, precious metal proofs only)	
4000 max	.925 sterling silver proof, price new	£60.00
1940 max	.925 sterling silver piedfort proof	£120.00
500 max	.917 gold proof	no data

COMMEMORATIVE TYPE 49c
THE BATTLE OF BRITAIN 1940
<u>**WITH DENOMINATION**</u>
Circulation issue, reverse as 49a
(Jody Clark portrait, with '50 PENCE', as shown)
(also dated 2019, see page 66)

For circulation issues the Royal Mint released these coins, which not only have the new Jody Clark 5th portrait of the Queen, they also have the denomination written as '50 PENCE' on the obverse.

		Used
2015 5,900,000	(5th portrait with '50 PENCE')	Face Value

27.3 mm • 8.0 grammes • cupro-nickel • plain edge

COMMEMORATIVE TYPE 50
BATTLE OF HASTINGS / 1066 / 2016
(Representation of a soldier inspired by the
Bayeux Tapestry)
Design by: John Bergdahl
(also dated 2019, see page 66)

		As-New	Proof
2016	6,700,000	£5.00	£18.00
21,718*	Specimen in folder	£12.00	
2,338 of 3k	.925 sterling silver proof		£50.00
1,469 of 1,500	.925 sterling silver piedfort proof		£60.00
237 of 350	.917 gold proof, price new		no data

* Plus 7,877 in packs with stamps and 5,139 BU coins in tubes (to other retailers).

COMMEMORATIVE TYPE 51
BEATRIX POTTER SERIES No.1,
BEATRIX POTTER
(Silhouette of Beatrix Potter, name, dates and
Peter Rabbit character)
Design by: Emma Noble

		UNC	As-New	Proof
2016	6,900,000	£1.00	£5.00	
61,658*	Specimen in pack		£12.00	
7,471	.925 sterling silver proof			£200.00
2,486	.925 sterling silver piedfort proof			£200.00
732	.917 gold proof			no data

* Plus 14,777 in sets of five Potter coins and 48,650 BU coins in tubes (to other retailers).

COMMEMORATIVE TYPE 52
BEATRIX POTTER SERIES, No.2,
PETER RABBIT
(The character Peter Rabbit, his name either side)
Design by: Emma Noble
Obverse: As Type 51

		UNC	As-New	Proof
2016	9,600,000 Standard, non-coloured coin	£1.00	£5.00	
	Standard, non-coloured coin. Extra left whisker, (die damage). **Used: £3.00**			
93,851	Standard, non-coloured coin in pack (+42,384 in tubes) £10.00			
14,995	.925 coloured sterling silver proof in clear Perspex box			£470.00
500	.925 coloured sterling silver proof in First Day Cover envelope			£400.00
250	.925 coloured sterling silver proof in black box (from Potter shops)			no data
250	.925 coloured sterling silver proof in cherry box + extras			no data

Despite the coins all being the same, the type of packaging and even the serial number (some people prefer very low numbers) can play a role with values! There are some variations to the values,
which seem to be down to the mood of buyers and the number on offer.

COMMEMORATIVE TYPE 53

BEATRIX POTTER SERIES, No. 3,
JEMIMA PUDDLE-DUCK
(The character Jemina Puddle-Duck, her name either side**)
Design by: Emma Noble
Obverse: As Type 51

		Used	As-New	Proof
2016	2,100,000 Standard, non-coloured coin	£9.00	£14.00	
54,929*	Standard, non-coloured coin in pack		£16.00	
14,921	.925 sterling silver proof in clear Perspex box			£140.00
250**	.925 sterling silver proof in black box			£140.00

* Plus 69,231 sold in tubes. ** Plus 750 in Royal Mail boxes.
The Puddle-Duck 50p is often seen with signs of 'die-clash', which results in outlines of the duck and/or the Queen appearing on the opposing side.

COMMEMORATIVE TYPE 54

BEATRIX POTTER SERIES, No. 4,
SQUIRREL NUTKIN
(The character Squirrel Nutkin, his name either side**)
Design by: Emma Noble
Obverse: As Type 51

		As-New	Proof
2016	5,000,000 Standard, non-coloured coin	£5.00	
45,884*	Standard, non-coloured coin in pack	£12.00	
15,000	.925 sterling silver proof in clear Perspex box		£70.00
250**	.925 sterling silver proof in black box		£90.00

** Plus 53,660 sold in tubes. ** Plus 750 in Royal Mail boxes.

COMMEMORATIVE TYPE 55

BEATRIX POTTER SERIES, No.5,
MRS TIGGY-WINKLE
(The character Mrs Tiggy-Winkle, her name either side**)
Design by: Emma Noble
Obverse: As Type 51

		As-New	Proof
2016	8,800,000 Standard, non-coloured coin	£5.00	
47,597*	Standard, non-coloured coin in pack (+52,937 in tubes)	£12.00	
14,893	.925 sterling silver proof in clear Perspex box		£65.00
250**	.925 sterling silver proof in black box		£90.00

* Plus 52,937 sold in tubes. * Plus 750 in Royal Mail boxes.

27.3 mm • 8.0 grammes • cupro-nickel • plain edge

COMMEMORATIVE TYPE 56
TEAM GB
(Swimmer, Team GB logo and Olympic rings)
Design by: Tim Sharp
Obverse: As Type 51

		As-New	Proof
2016	6,400,000	£6.00	
34,162*	Specimen in folder	£8.00	
3,956 of 4k*	.925 sterling silver proof		£30.00
1,296 of 2,016	.925 sterling silver piedfort proof		£55.00
302 of 306	.917 gold proof		£550.00

* Plus 500 silver proof in capsules and 8,484 'BU' coins in tubes for other retailers.

COMMEMORATIVE TYPE 57
SIR ISAAC NEWTON
(Rings and ellipses around the sun /
SIR ISAAC NEWTON above,
FIFTY PENCE below)
Design by: Aaron West

		Used	As-New	Proof
2017 (57A)	1,801,500 (many exist with die-clash)	£3.00	£7.00	
54,057	Specimen in folder		£15.00	
4,000 max.	.925 sterling silver proof			£55.00
3,000 max.	.925 sterling silver piedfort proof			£75.00
500 max.	.917 gold proof			£750.00
2018 (57B)	Dated 2018, 'Strike Your Own' in card package.		£30.00	

See also page 166 for more info on the 'Strike Your Own' coins.

COMMEMORATIVE TYPE 58
THE TALE OF PETER RABBIT
BEATRIX POTTER SERIES, No.6
(Peter Rabbit walking right with the title text
surrounding him)
Design by: Emma Noble
Obverse: As Type 51, dated 2017

		UNC	As-New	Proof
2017	19,900,000	£1.00	£5.00	
221,866*	Specimen in folder, price new		£10.00	
30k max.*	.925 coloured sterling silver proof in clear Perspex box			£30.00
3,150 max.*	.925 coloured sterling silver proof in black box (various)			£30.00
3,500 max.*	.925 coloured sterling silver proof in large box with book			£60.00
450 max.	.917 gold proof, 15.5g in large box with book			£800.00

* The Specimen in folders figures for all 2017 Beatrix Potter coins also include coins sold to retailers in tubes.

A max. figure of 40k for the total silver proofs was quoted on the Royal Mint website.

COMMEMORATIVE TYPE 59
MR JEREMY FISHER
BEATRIX POTTER SERIES, No.7
(The character Mr Jeremy Fisher, his name to the left)
Design by: Emma Noble
Obverse: As Type 51, dated 2017

		UNC	As-New	Proof
2017	9,900,000	£1.00	£5.00	
165,668*	Specimen in folder, price new		£9.00	
30k max.*	.925 coloured sterling silver proof in clear Perspex box			£25.00
500 max.*	.925 coloured sterling silver proof in black box (various)			£25.00
3,500 max.*	.925 coloured sterling silver proof in large box with book			£60.00

* A max. figure of 40k quoted, see notes for coin type 58.

COMMEMORATIVE TYPE 60
TOM KITTEN
BEATRIX POTTER SERIES, No.8
(The character Tom Kitten facing, his name flanking him)
Design by: Emma Noble
Obverse: As Type 51, dated 2017

		As-New	Proof
2017	9,500,000	£5.00	
159,302*	Specimen in folder	£9.00	
30k max.*	.925 coloured sterling silver proof in clear Perspex box		£28.00
500 max.*	.925 coloured sterling silver proof in black box (various)		£28.00
3,500 max.*	.925 coloured sterling silver proof in large box with book		£50.00

* A max. figure of 40k quoted, see notes for coin type 58.

COMMEMORATIVE TYPE 61
BENJAMIN BUNNY
BEATRIX POTTER SERIES, No.9
(The character Benjamin Bunny, facing his name flanking him)
Design by: Emma Noble
Obverse: As Type 51, dated 2017

		As-New	Proof
2017	25,000,000	£5.00	
158,022*	Specimen in folder	£7.00	
30k max.*	.925 coloured sterling silver proof in clear Perspex box		£32.00
500 max.*	.925 coloured sterling silver proof in black box (various)		£32.00
3,500 max.*	.925 coloured sterling silver proof in large box with book		£50.00

* A max. figure of 40k quoted, see notes for coin type 58.

27.3 mm • 8.0 grammes • cupro-nickel • plain edge

COMMEMORATIVE TYPE 62
REPRESENTATION OF THE PEOPLE ACT
(Group of people with '1918 REPRESENTATION OF THE
PEOPLE ACT' above them)
Design by: Stephen Taylor
Obverse: As Type 51, dated 2018

		As-New	Proof
2018	9,000,000	£4.00	£12.00
	Specimen in folder	£10.00	
3,500 max.	.925 sterling silver proof		£40.00
1,918 max.	.925 sterling silver piedfort proof		£60.00
300 max.	.917 gold proof		£750.00

See also coin 57, for the 2018 dated Isaac Newton 50p.

COMMEMORATIVE TYPE 63
PETER RABBIT (late February 2018)
BEATRIX POTTER SERIES, No.10
(Peter Rabbit eating radishes)
Design by: Emma Noble
Obverse: As Type 51, dated 2018

		Used	As-New	Proof
2018	1,400,000	£5.50	£8.00	
	Specimen in folder		£9.00	
35k max.	.925 coloured sterling silver proof			£28.00
3,500 max.	As above, in box with book			£60.00
450 max.	.917 gold proof, in box with book, price new			£1,000.00

COMMEMORATIVE TYPE 64
FLOPSY BUNNY (March 2018)
BEATRIX POTTER SERIES, No.11
(Flopsy Bunny looking right)
Design by: Emma Noble
Obverse: As Type 51, dated 2018

		Used	As-new	Proof
2018	1,400,000	£6.00	£10.00	
	Specimen in folder		£10.00	
30k max.	.925 coloured sterling silver proof			£28.00
3,500 max.	As above, in box with book			£60.00

COMMEMORATIVE TYPE 65
THE TAILOR OF GLOUCESTER (April 2018)
BEATRIX POTTER SERIES, No.11
(Helpful little mouse reading a newspaper)
Design by: Emma Noble
Obverse: As Type 51, dated 2018

		Used	As-New	Proof
2018	3,900,000	£1.50	£4.00	
	Specimen in folder		£7.00	
30k max.	.925 coloured sterling silver proof, price new			£32.00
3,500 max.	As above, in box with book			£60.00

COMMEMORATIVE TYPE 66
MRS TITTLEMOUSE (May 2018)
BEATRIX POTTER SERIES, No.12
(Mrs Tittlemouse facing left)
Design by: Emma Noble
Obverse: As Type 51, dated 2018

		Used	As-New	Proof
2018	1,700,000	£3.00	£6.00	
	Specimen in folder		£10.00	
30k max.	.925 coloured sterling silver proof			£28.00
3,500 max.	As above, in box with book			£60.00

COMMEMORATIVE TYPE 67
PADDINGTON BEAR 60th ANNIVERSARY (1 of 4)
(Paddington bear sitting at Paddington Station)
Design by: David Knapton
Obverse: As Type 51, dated 2018

		As-New	Proof
2018	5,001,000	£5.00	£5.00
	Specimen in folder, price new	£10.00	
60k max.	.925 coloured sterling silver proof		£50.00
600 max.	.917 gold proof		£900.00

27.3 mm • 8.0 grammes • cupro-nickel • plain edge

COMMEMORATIVE TYPE 68
PADDINGTON BEAR 60th ANNIVERSARY (2 of 4)
(Paddington bear waving flag, Buckingham palace in background)
Design by: David Knapton
Obverse: As Type 51, dated 2018

		As-New	Proof
2018	5,901,000	£5.00	
	Specimen in folder, price new	£10.00	
60k max.	.925 coloured sterling silver proof		£50.00
600 max.	.917 gold proof		£800.00

COMMEMORATIVE TYPE 69
RAYMOND BRIGGS' 'SNOWMAN' 40th ANNIVERSARY
(Snowman and boy flying)
Design by: Natasha Ratcliffe
Obverse: As Type 51, dated 2018
Note that another Snowman coin appeared in 2019 (TYPE 79)

		As-New	Proof
2018	(not put into general circulation)	£14.00	
	Specimen in folder	£15.00	
15k max.	.925 coloured sterling silver proof		£50.00
400 max.	.917 gold proof		£1,000.00

The 2019 retrospective 50th Anniversary set, part one (British Culture).

In a similar fashion to 2009 for the 40th anniversary of the 50p coin, the Royal Mint released sets of 50p coins for the 50th anniversary. This time around the reverse types seem to have been chosen fairly randomly.

Despite it being made clear from the outset that both sets of five coins would only be available to buy in proof form, they were also sold as BU sets a few weeks later - this no doubt facilitated a hefty wedge of extra profit in it for the Royal Mint and there were quite a few disappointed people who had bought the proof sets, only to find out later on that their coins were not so elusive.

The first set of five different coins included the following:

The obverses are shown first, matched to the five different reverses. The original reverse designs for three of the coins (right) already include the face value, and for that reason an obverse type with just the date and no '50 PENCE' has been used.

Set of 5 'British Culture' themed fifty pence coins, comprising:

NEW PENCE Britannia* (original REVERSE 1), Kew Gardens (TYPE 13), the Four Minute Mile (TYPE 8), Scouting (TYPE 12) and Girlguiding (TYPE 15).

		As-New	Proof
	Base metal 'Uncirculated' set	£40.00	
3,500	Base metal proof set		£90.00
1,969	Silver proof set		£190.00
1,220	Silver piedfort proof set, price new		£450.00
75	Gold proof set, price new		£3,825.00
50	Gold piedfort proof set, price new		£9,370.00

All of the above proof set versions sold out very quickly (before people knew they would also appear in non-proof form) and a lot appeared - instantly - on eBay and other online sales platforms. At the time of writing the base metal uncirculated sets are still on sale. Many sets have been split for the Kew Gardens coin, as it's a cheaper way of filling the gap, instead of sourcing an original 2009 coin - for this reason the Kew on its own tends to be more expensive than the others. Another set of five different coins appeared later in 2019, see page 66.

*The coin with the Britannia 'NEW PENCE' type reverse was also made available as a 'Strike Your Own' (so, roughly BU quality) at the beginning of 2019 (see next page).

COMMEMORATIVE TYPE 70
SIR ARTHUR CONAN DOYLE
(Silhouette of Sherlock Holmes, book titles flanking him)
Design by: Stephen Raw
Obverse: As Type 57, dated 2019

		As-New	Proof
2019			
	(circulated in large numbers - also an SYO, see p.166)	£5.00	£7.00
7,500 max	.925 sterling silver proof		£70.00
2,500 max	.925 sterling silver piedfort proof, price new		£80.00
250 max	.917 gold proof		£1,200.00

STRIKE YOUR OWN (TYPE 71)
NEW PENCE BRITANNIA REVERSE
(The original 50p reverse, used 1969 - 1981)
Design by: Christopher Ironside

		As-New
2019	Available as a 'Strike Your Own' only	£19.00

See also page 166 for more info on the 'Strike Your Own' coins.

COMMEMORATIVE TYPE 72
THE GRUFFALO (1 of 2)
(The Gruffalo facing right, his name above)
Design by: Axel Scheffler (Magic Light Pictures Ltd)
Obverse: As Type 71

		As-New	Proof
2019	(not put into general circulation)	£5.00	
	Specimen in folder, price new	£10.00	
25k max.*	.925 coloured sterling silver proof		£60-£70
600 max.	.917 gold proof, price new		£795.00

* Plus another 5,000 allocated to other presentations, potentially Royal Mail packages etc. Various other presentation / gift packs were sold.

COMMEMORATIVE TYPE 73
STEPHEN HAWKING (Innovation in Science series)
(Representation of a black hole with an equation and his name)
Design by: Edwina Ellis
Obverse: As Type 71

		As-New	Proof
2019	(not put into general circulation)	£5.00	
	Specimen in folder, price new	£10.00	
5,500 max	.925 sterling silver proof, price new		£55.00
2,500 max	.925 sterling silver piedfort proof, price new		£95.00
400 max	.917 gold proof, price new		£980.00

COMMEMORATIVE TYPE 74
PETER RABBIT
Design by: Emma Noble
(Peter Rabbit again)
Obverse: As Type 71

		As-New	Proof
2019	(not put into general circulation)	£5.00	
	Specimen in folder, price new	£10.00	
30k max	.925 sterling silver proof (with colour), price new		£65.00
500 max	.917 gold proof, price new		£980.00

COMMEMORATIVE TYPE 75
PADDINGTON BEAR 60th ANNIVERSARY? (3 of 4)
(Paddington bear wearing coat, Tower of London in back-
ground)
Design by: David Knapton
Obverse: As Type 71

		As-New	Proof
2019	(circulated in large numbers)	£5.00	
	Specimen in folder, price new	£10.00	
25k max	.925 sterling silver proof (with colour), price new		£65.00
600 max	.917 gold proof, price new		£1,020.00

27.3 mm • 8.0 grammes • cupro-nickel • plain edge

The 2019 retrospective 50th Anniversary set, part two (British Military).

This is the second set of five different loosely themed coins. It includes the following:

The obverses are shown first, matched to the five different reverses. The original reverse designs for three of the coins (right) already include the face value, and for that reason an obverse type with just the date and no '50 PENCE' has been used.

Set of 5 'British Military' themed fifty pence coins, comprising: D-Day (TYPE 3), Victoria Cross award and acts (TYPES 10 & 11), Battle of Britain (TYPE 49) and the Battle of Hastings (TYPE 50).

		As-New	Proof
	Base metal 'Uncirculated' set	£35.00	
3,500	Base metal proof set		£60.00
1,969	Silver proof set		£150.00
1,220	Silver piedfort proof set, price new		£450.00
75	Gold proof set, price new		£3,825.00
50	Gold piedfort proof set, price new		£9,370.00

COMMEMORATIVE TYPE 76
PADDINGTON BEAR 60th ANNIVERSARY? (4 of 4)
(Paddington doffing hat, St. Paul's Cathedral in background)
Design by: David Knapton
Obverse: As Type 71

		As-New	Proof
2019	(circulated in large numbers)	£5.00	
	Specimen in folder, price new	£10.00	
25k max	.925 sterling silver proof (with colour), price new		£65.00
600 max	.917 gold proof, price new		£1,020.00

COMMEMORATIVE TYPE 77
GRUFFALO (2 of 2)
(The second Gruffalo commemorative)
Design by: Magic Light Pictures
Obverse: As Type 71

		As-New	Proof
2019	(not put into general circulation)	£5.00	
	Specimen in folder, price new	£10.00	
25k max	.925 sterling silver proof (with colour), price new		£65.00
600 max	.917 gold proof, price new		£1,020.00

COMMEMORATIVE TYPE 78
BRITANNIA with mint mark and lettered angles
(Re-issue of the original 50p design, 50 years after its first use)
Design by: Christopher Ironside (in the 1960s)
Obverse: As Type 71

		As-New	Proof
2019	(not put into general circulation)	£5.00	
	Specimen in folder, price new	£10.00	
3,500 max	.925 sterling silver proof, price new		£55.00
1,969 max	.925 sterling silver piedfort proof, price new		£95.00
300 max	.917 gold proof, price new		£945.00

COMMEMORATIVE TYPE 79
SNOWMAN 2
Design by: Snowman Enterprises
(Another Snowman coin, issued about a
year after the first - Type 69)
Obverse: As Type 71

		As-New	Proof
2019	(not put into general circulation)	£5.00	
	Specimen in folder, price new	£10.00	
25k max	.925 sterling silver proof (with colour), price new		£65.00
600 max	.917 gold proof, price new		£1,020.00

COMMEMORATIVE TYPE 80
WALLACE & GROMIT
Design by: Nick Park
(To mark the 30th anniversary of Wallace & Gromit)
Obverse: As Type 71

		As-New	Proof
2019	(not put into general circulation)	£5.00	
	Specimen in folder, price new	£10.00	
25k max	.925 sterling silver proof (with colour), price new		£65.00
630 max	.917 gold proof, price new		£1,020.00

COMMEMORATIVE TYPE 81
TEAM GB
Design by: David Knapton
(In support of Team GB at the 2020 Tokyo Olympics)
Obverse: As Type 71, dated 2020

		As-New	Proof
2020	Only available in sets at the time of writing	£30.00*	

*They were higher at one stage! Due to the novel corona-virus pandemic, the Tokyo 2020 Olympic games has been re-scheduled to take place in 2021. This caused speculation on this coin - even though when it does happen it will still be called 'Tokyo 2020' and despite the fact that the coins are still available to buy new (within BU and proof sets). I suspect that as long as there is demand, the Royal Mint will keep producing them and will no doubt enjoy bumper sales due to the speculation and usual eBay nonsense. Maybe they will produce a 2021 dated version next year to cash in for a second time - who knows.

COMMEMORATIVE TYPE 82

BREXIT

Design by: Royal Mint in-house
(Withdrawal from the European Union)
Obverse: As Type 71, dated 2020

		Used	As-New	Proof
2020	Millions circulated	FV		
	Specimen in folder, price new		£10.00	
5,000	Specimen in folder with a 1973 EEC entry 50p*		£60.00	
47k max	.925 sterling silver proof, price new			£60.00
1,500 max	.917 gold proof, price new			£1,020.00

* The 1973 coins have been sourced second hand and many I've seen have been in unremarkable condition, despite them being described as 'Brilliant Uncirculated' on the back of the packs.

COMMEMORATIVE TYPE 83

DINOSAURIA (1 of 3)

Design by: Robert Nicholls
(Megalosaurus - one of three Dinosauria themed coins)
Obverse: As Type 71, dated 2020

		As-New	Proof
2020	(not put into general circulation)	£5.00	
	Specimen in folder, price new	£10.00	
50k max	Specimen in folder with added colour, price new	£20.00	
3k max	.925 sterling silver proof, price new		£60.00
7k max	.925 sterling silver proof with added colour, price new		£65.00
350 max	.917 gold proof, price new		£1,020.00

COMMEMORATIVE TYPE 84

DINOSAURIA (2 of 3)

Design by: Robert Nicholls
(Iguanodon - one of three Dinosauria themed coins)
Obverse: As Type 71, dated 2020

		As-New	Proof
2020	(not put into general circulation)	£5.00	
	Specimen in folder, price new	£10.00	
50k max	Specimen in folder with added colour, price new	£20.00	
3k max	.925 sterling silver proof, price new		£60.00
7k max	.925 sterling silver proof with added colour, price new		£65.00
350 max	.917 gold proof, price new		£1,020.00

27.3 mm • 8.0 grammes • cupro-nickel • plain edge

COMMEMORATIVE TYPE 85
PETER RABBIT
Design by: Emma Noble
(Peter Rabbit, again. Squeezing under a gate)
Obverse: As Type 71, dated 2020

		As-New	Proof
2020	(not put into general circulation)	£5.00	
	Specimen in folder, price new	£10.00	
14,500 max	.925 sterling silver proof (with colour), price new		£60.00
500 max	.917 gold proof, price new		£1,020.00

No image yet.

COMMEMORATIVE TYPE 86
DINOSAURIA (3 of 3)
Design by: Robert Nicholls
(Hylaeosaurus - one of three Dinosauria themed coins)
Obverse: As Type 71, dated 2020

		As-New	Proof
2020	(not to be put into general circulation)	TBC	
	Specimen in folder, price new	£10?	
	Specimen in folder with added colour, price new	TBC	
	.925 sterling silver proof, price new		TBC
	.925 sterling silver proof with added colour, price new		TBC
	.917 gold proof, price new		TBC

No image yet.

COMMEMORATIVE TYPE 87
ROSALIND FRANKLIN (Innovation in Science series)
Design by:
(Currently no further details)
Obverse: ?

		As-New	Proof
2020	(not to be put into general circulation)	TBC	
	Specimen in folder, price new	£10?	
	Specimen in folder with added colour, price new	TBC	
	.925 sterling silver proof, price new		TBC
	.925 sterling silver proof with added colour, price new		TBC
	.917 gold proof, price new		TBC

What's currently legal tender?

Only the new (post 2016) 12-sided pound coins are legal tender. None of the old round pound coins can be spent, but they can be credited into most UK bank accounts.

Correct edge lettering for the year and what they mean

The following old pound coins have the edge inscription DECUS ET TUTAMEN (Latin for 'An ornament and a safeguard'):

1983 (UK theme), 1986 (NI theme), 1987 (English theme), 1988 (UK theme), 1991 (NI theme), 1992 (English theme), 1993 (UK theme), 1996 (NI theme), 1997 (English theme), 1998 (UK theme), 2001 (NI theme), 2002 (English theme), 2003 (UK theme), 2008 (UK theme) and the standard definitive shield reverse coins made from 2008 to 2016 The 2013 English floral theme coin, the 2014 Northern Ireland floral theme coin as well as the 2015 Royal Arms coin and the 2016 Heraldic last round pound also carry the DECUS ET TUTAMEN edge inscription.

Scottish theme coins (dated 1984, 1989, 1994, 1999 and 2014) have the inscription 'NEMO ME IMPUNE LACESSIT' (Latin for 'No-one provokes me with impunity').

Welsh theme coins (dated 1985, 1990, 1995, 2000 and 2013) have the inscription 'PLEIDIOL WYF I'M GWLAD' (Welsh for 'True I am to my country').

The bridge themed coins (dated 2004, 2005, 2006 and 2007) have a patterned edge with no edge lettering.

The capital city themed coins have the following edge inscriptions:

2010, Belfast - 'PRO TANTO QUID RETRIBUAMUS' (what shall we give in return for so much).
2010, London - 'DOMINE DIRIGE NOS' (Lord, direct us).
2011, Cardiff - 'Y DDRAIG GOCH DDYRY CYCHWYN' (the red dragon inspires action).
2011, Edinburgh - 'NISI DOMINUS FRUSTRA' (without the Lord, in vain)

Which are hard to find?

Now they have been removed from every day use all of the old pounds are harder to find, but none are rare. The most expensive old £1 coins are currently 1998, 1999, the 2015 with shield reverse (and 5th portrait of the Queen), the 2016 with shield reverse and the 2016 heraldic beasts coin as they were all only made for year sets or packages and so had to be purchased originally. In the future though, it probably won't really matter, as even where the coins that were only sold in packs are concerned, there are plenty to go round. Historically when a coin type is removed from circulation, the interest in them dwindles rapidly.

The 1988 has a popular design and relatively low mintage of just over seven million which doesn't make it rare, but it's certainly the scarcest in comparison to most of the other earlier coins. The 2011 Edinburgh coin has a mintage of under one million and often sells for a little more than face value, even in used condition. The other capital cities coins and the floral themed coins are popular.

71

OBVERSES

OBVERSE 1
(used 1983 & 1984)
D•G•REG•F•D•(date) || ELIZABETH II
Elizabeth II, Dei Gratia Regina, Fidei Defensor
(Elizabeth II, By the Grace of God Queen and Defender of the Faith)
Portrait by: Arnold Machin

OBVERSE 2
(used 1985 - 1997)
ELIZABETH II || D•G•REG•F•D•(date)
Elizabeth II, Dei Gratia Regina, Fidei Defensor
(Elizabeth II, By the Grace of God Queen and Defender of the Faith)
Portrait by: Raphael Maklouf

OBVERSE 3
(used 1998 - 2008)
ELIZABETH II•D•G || REG•F•D•(date)
Elizabeth II, Dei Gratia Regina, Fidei Defensor
(Elizabeth II, By the Grace of God Queen and Defender of the Faith)
Portrait by: Ian Rank-Broadley

OBVERSE 4 (similar to last, with no rim beading)
(used 2008 to 2015)
ELIZABETH II•D•G || REG•F•D•(date)
Elizabeth II, Dei Gratia Regina, Fidei Defensor
(Elizabeth II, By the Grace of God Queen and Defender of the Faith)
Portrait by: Ian Rank-Broadley

OBVERSE 5
(used 2015 and 2016 on old type £1 coins)
ELIZABETH II•D•G || REG•F•D•(date)
Elizabeth II, Dei Gratia Regina, Fidei Defensor
(Elizabeth II, By the Grace of God Queen and Defender of the Faith)
Portrait by: Jody Clark

1983 — UK Royal Arms design by Eric Sewell
Edge: DECUS ET TUTAMEN

		UNC	As-New	Proof
443,053,510		£2.50	£5.00	£6.00
	Specimen in folder		£9.00	
50,000	.925 sterling silver proof			£25.00
10,000	.925 sterling silver piedfort proof			£60.00

The following 4 coins ("Coronet" series) were designed by Leslie Durbin.

1984 — Scottish Thistle in Coronet.
Edge: NEMO ME IMPUNE LACESSIT

		UNC	As-New	Proof
146,256,501		£3.00	£5.00	£6.00
27,960	Specimen in folder		£9.00	
44,855	.925 sterling silver proof			£20.00
15,000	.925 sterling silver piedfort proof			£35.00

1985 — Welsh Leek in Coronet. Edge: PLEIDIOL WYF I'M GWLAD

		UNC	As-New	Proof
228,430,749		£3.00	£5.00	£6.00
24,850	Specimen in folder		£9.00	
50,000	.925 sterling silver proof			£20.00
15,000	.925 sterling silver piedfort proof			£25.00

1986 — N.I. Flax in Coronet. Edge: DECUS ET TUTAMEN

		UNC	As-New	Proof
10,409,501		£3.00	£5.00	£6.00
19,908	Specimen in folder		£9.00	
37,958	.925 sterling silver proof			£20.00
15,000	.925 sterling silver piedfort proof			£25.00

1987 — English Oak in Coronet. Edge: DECUS ET TUTAMEN

		UNC	As-New	Proof
39,298,502		£3.00	£5.00	£6.00
72,607	Specimen in folder		£9.00	
50,500	.925 sterling silver proof			£20.00
15,000	.925 sterling silver piedfort proof			£22.00

1988   Royal Shield design (UK) by Derek Gorringe
Edge: DECUS ET TUTAMEN

		UNC	As-New	Proof
7,118,825	Used: £2.00	£3.00	£5.00	£8.00
29,550	Specimen in folder		£6.00	
50,000	.925 sterling silver proof			£20.00
10,000	.925 sterling silver piedfort proof			£22.00

The following 4 coins ("Coronet" series) were designed by Leslie Durbin.

1989   Scottish Thistle in Coronet.
Edge: NEMO ME IMPUNE LACESSIT

		UNC	As-New	Proof
70,580,501		£3.00	£5.00	£5.00
25,000	.925 sterling silver proof			£12.00
10,000	.925 sterling silver piedfort proof			£20.00

1990   Welsh Leek in Coronet. Edge: PLEIDIOL WYF I'M GWLAD

97,269,302		£3.00	£5.00	£5.00
25,000	.925 sterling silver proof			£18.00

1991   N.I. Flax in Coronet. Edge: DECUS ET TUTAMEN

38,443,575		£3.00	£5.00	£8.00
25,000	.925 sterling silver proof			£18.00

1992   English Oak in Coronet. Edge: DECUS ET TUTAMEN

36,320,487		£3.00	£5.00	£5.00
25,000	.925 sterling silver proof			£18.00

1993	UK Royal Arms design by Eric Sewell Edge: DECUS ET TUTAMEN	UNC	As-New	Proof
114,744,500		£3.00	£5.00	£6.00
50,000	.925 sterling silver proof			£18.00
10,000	.925 sterling silver piedfort proof			£20.00

The following 4 coins ("Heraldic" series) were designed by Norman Sillman.

1994	Scottish Lion Rampant. Edge: NEMO ME IMPUNE LACESSIT			
29,752,525		£2.00	£5.00	£8.00
	Specimen in folder		£8.00	
25,000	.925 sterling silver proof			£15.00
11,722	.925 sterling silver piedfort proof			£20.00

1995	Welsh Dragon. Edge: PLEIDIOL WYF I'M GWLAD			
34,503,501		£2.00	£5.00	£7.00
	Specimen in folder		£7.00	
	Specimen in folder (Welsh text)		no data	
27,445	.925 sterling silver proof			£20.00
8,458	.925 sterling silver piedfort proof			£25.00

1996	N.I. Celtic Cross. Edge: DECUS ET TUTAMEN			
89,886,000		£2.00	£5.00	£7.00
	Specimen in folder		£10.00	
25,000	.925 sterling silver cased proof			£20.00
10,000	.925 sterling silver piedfort cased proof			£25.00

1997	English Three Lions. Edge: DECUS ET TUTAMEN			
57,117,450		£2.00	£5.00	£7.00
56,996	Specimen in folder		£8.00	
20,137	.925 sterling silver proof			£20.00
10,000	.925 sterling silver piedfort proof			£25.00

1998 — UK Royal Arms design by Eric Sewell
Edge: DECUS ET TUTAMEN

		UNC	As-New	Proof
(BU packs only) **Used: £15.00**			£20.00	£20.00
13,863	.925 sterling silver proof			£25.00
10,000	.925 sterling silver piedfort proof			£30.00

1999 — Scottish Lion Rampant. Edge: NEMO ME IMPUNE LACESSIT

			As-New	Proof
(BU packs only) **Used: £16.00**			£20.00	£25.00
25,000	.925 sterling silver proof			£20.00
2,000	.925 sterling "Special Frosted Finish" proof			£20.00
10,000	.925 sterling silver piedfort proof			£25.00

2000 — Welsh Dragon. Edge: PLEIDIOL WYF I'M GWLAD

		UNC	As-New	Proof
109,496,500		£2.00	£5.00	£8.00
40,000	.925 sterling silver proof			£20.00
2,000	.925 sterling "Special Frosted Finish" proof			£25.00
10,000	.925 sterling silver piedfort proof			£25.00

2001 — N.I. Celtic Cross. Edge: DECUS ET TUTAMEN

		UNC	As-New	Proof
58,093,731		£2.00	£5.00	£8.00
13,237	.925 sterling silver proof			£25.00
2,000	.925 sterling "Special Frosted Finish" proof			£35.00
8,464	.925 sterling silver piedfort proof			£25.00

2002 — English Three Lions. Edge: DECUS ET TUTAMEN

		UNC	As-New	Proof
77,818,000		£2.00	£5.00	£8.00
17,693	.925 sterling silver proof			£20.00
2,000	.925 sterling "Special Frosted Finish" proof			£25.00
6,599	.925 sterling silver piedfort proof			£25.00

2003 — UK Royal Arms design by Eric Sewell
Edge: DECUS ET TUTAMEN

		UNC	As-New	Proof
61,596,500		£2.00	£5.00	£8.00
15,830	.925 sterling silver proof			£20.00
9,871	.925 sterling silver piedfort proof			£25.00

2003 dated Bridges 'PATTERN' set of 4 coins (one shown to left)

7,500 max .925 sterling silver proofs, edge hallmarked	£70.00
3,000 max .917 gold proofs, edge hall marked	£2,300.00

2004 dated Heraldic beasts 'PATTERN' set of 4 coins (proof only)

5,000 max .925 sterling silver proofs, edge hallmarked	£90.00
2,250 max .917 gold proofs, edge hallmarked	£2,300.00

The following 4 coins ("Bridge" series) were designed by Edwina Ellis. The edges all feature a decorative pattern.

2004   Scotland - Forth Bridge

		UNC	As-New	Proof
39,162,000		£3.00	£6.00	£11.00
24,014	Specimen in folder		£15.00	
11,470	.925 sterling silver proof			£20.00
7,013	.925 sterling silver piedfort cased proof			£25.00
2,618	.917 gold proof			£500.00

2005   Wales - Menai Bridge

		UNC	As-New	Proof
99,429,500		£3.00	£6.00	£11.00
24,802	Specimen in folder		£15.00	
8,371	.925 sterling silver proof			£20.00
6,007	.925 sterling silver piedfort cased proof			£25.00
1,195	.917 gold proof			£500.00

Also sold in packs with the 2005 £2 (Gunpowder plot) and 2005 50p (Johnson's Dictionary). Value: £20

2006   Northern Ireland - Egyptian Arch

		UNC	As-New	Proof
38,938,000		£3.00	£6.00	£11.00
23,856	Specimen in folder		£15.00	
14,765	.925 sterling silver proof			£20.00
5,129	.925 sterling silver piedfort cased proof			£25.00
728	.917 gold proof			£550.00

2007   England - Millennium Bridge

		UNC	As-New	Proof
26,180,160		£3.00	£6.00	£11.00
5,326	Specimen in folder		£15.00	
10,110	.925 sterling silver proof			£20.00
5,739	.925 sterling silver piedfort cased proof			£25.00
1,122	.917 gold proof			£550.00

2008 — UK Royal Arms design by: Eric Sewell. With Obverse 3.
Edge: DECUS ET TUTAMEN

		UNC	As-New	Proof
3,910,000	(BU packs: 18,336)　Used: £2.00	£5.00	£10.00	£10.00
9,134	.925 sterling silver proof			£20.00
7,894	.925 sterling silver piedfort cased proof			£30.00
2,005	Set of 14 £1 coins, all designs 1983 - 2008. Silver with gold coloured 'silhouette' details. All dated 2008			£300.00
	As above, as gold proof set			no data

Large shield part of the UK Royal coat of Arms by: Matthew Dent. With Obverse 4 or 5.

		UNC	As-New	Proof
2008	43,827,300	£2.00	£7.00	£10.00
5,000	.925 sterling silver proof			£35.00
2,456	.925 sterling piedfort proof			£50.00
860	.917 gold proof			£700.00
2009	27,625,600	£2.00	£7.00	£10.00
	.925 sterling silver proof from set			£30.00
	.917 gold proof			£600.00
2010	57,120,000	£2.00	£7.00	£10.00
	Silver proofs sold in sets only			
2011	25,415,000	£2.00	£7.00	£10.00
	Silver proofs sold in sets only			
2012	35,700,030	£2.00	£7.00	£10.00
1,234	.925 sterling silver proof			no data
	.925 silver BU			no data
	Also seen as silver proof with gold plated shield detail			
2013	13,090,500	£2.00	£7.00	£10.00
	.925 sterling silver proof (available in sets only)			no data
	.925 silver 'Royal Birth' BU (4,414 of 10k max)			£30.00?
	.917 gold proof (17 sold, plus 59 in sets)			no data
2014	79,305,200	£2.00	£7.00	£10.00
	.925 sterling silver proof (available in sets only)			£40.00
750	.925 sterling silver BU			no data
2015	29,580,000 (Obverse 4)	£2.00	£7.00	£10.00
	(Obverse 5) (in sets only, 23,643 total)		£20.00	£20.00
	Silver proofs sold in sets only			no data
2016	Available in sets only (30,205 total)		£24.00	£25.00

The following 4 coins ("Capital Cities" series) were designed by Stuart Devlin and all use Obverse 4.

2010 Belfast

Edge: PRO TANTO QUID RETRIBUAMUS

	Used	As-New	Proof
6,205,000 (BU packs: 6,767)	£2.00	£15.00	£15.00
.925 sterling silver proof			£25.00
.925 sterling silver piedfort proof			£30.00

2010 London

Edge: DOMINE DIRIGE NOS

	Used	As-New	Proof
2,635,000 (BU packs: 8,584)	£3.00	£15.00*	£15.00
.925 sterling silver proof			£25.00
.925 sterling silver piedfort proof			£40.00

* Some of the BU packs contained the 2010 Shield reverse coin in error.

4,023 BU packs containing both 2010 coins were sold.

2011 Cardiff

Edge: Y DDRAIG GOCH DDYRY CYCHWYN

	Used	As-New	Proof
1,615,000	£3.00	£25.00	£25.00
.925 sterling silver proof (5,553 sold)			£30.00
.925 sterling silver piedfort proof (1,615 sold)			£35.00
.917 gold proof (524 sold)			no data

Incorrect die alignment (rotated over 90 degrees) Cardiff coins noted.

2011 Edinburgh

Edge: NISI DOMINUS FRUSTRA

	Used	As-New	Proof
935,000	£5.00	£30.00	£30.00
.925 sterling silver proof (4,973 sold)			£40.00
.925 sterling silver piedfort proof (2,696 sold)			£50.00
.917 gold proof (499 sold)			no data

3,198 BU packs containing both 2011 coins were sold.

2013   National Floral Symbols series - England, by Timothy Noad
Edge: DECUS ET TUTAMEN

		UNC	As-New	Proof
	5,270,000	£2.00	£4.00	£10.00
1,858	.925 sterling silver proof*			£40.00
1,071	.925 sterling silver piedfort proof			£50.00
185	.917 gold proof (plus 99 in sets with Wales)			no data

2013   National Floral Symbols series - Wales by Timothy Noad
Edge: PLEIDIOL WYF I'M GWLAD

		UNC	As-New	Proof
	5,270,000	£2.00	£4.00	£10.00
1,618	.925 sterling silver proof*			£40.00
860	.925 sterling silver piedfort proof			£50.00
175	.917 gold proof (plus 99 in sets with England)			-

This coin also exists with incorrect (rotated) die alignment.
* Plus an additional 1,476 2013 silver proof coins sold in pairs.
6,112 BU packs of both 2013 coins were sold.

? 2013 Silver proof version of the 1988 design			£100.00
? 2013 Silver proof version of the 1983 design			£100.00

2014   National Floral Symbols series - Scotland, by Timothy Noad
Edge: NEMO ME IMPUNE LACESSIT

		UNC	As-New	Proof
	5,185,000	£2.00	£4.00	£12.00
1,540	.925 sterling silver proof			£50.00
	.925 sterling silver piedfort proof			£70.00?
154	.917 gold proof			no data

2014   National Floral Symbols series - N. Ireland, by Timothy Noad
Edge: DECUS ET TUTAMEN

		UNC	As-New	Proof
	5,780,000	£2.00	£4.00	£12.00
1,502	.925 sterling silver proof			£50.00
788	.925 sterling silver piedfort proof			£70.00?
166	.917 gold proof			no data

3,832 BU packs of both 2014 coins were sold.

2015   The Royal Arms - by Timothy Noad
Edge: DECUS ET TUTAMEN

		UNC	As-New	Proof
All with Obverse 5				
	129,616,985	£2.00	£4.00	
9,294	BU pack		£15.00	
3,500 max	.925 sterling silver proof			£60.00
2,000 max	.925 sterling piedfort proof			£150.00?
500 max	.917 gold proof (price new £850)			no data

2016   Four Heraldic beast symbols of the UK -
by Gregory Cameron, Bishop of St Asaph.
'The last round pound'. Edge: DECUS ET TUTAMEN

		BU	Proof
96,089	Non-circulated, had to be purchased*	£15.00	£20.00
7,491	.925 sterling silver proof		£40.00
2,993	.925 sterling piedfort proof		£120.00?
499	.917 gold proof		no data

*These coins were also sold in pairs (9,850 total) - combined with a cross-crosslet mint marked new pound coin. This coin and the new pound were also sold as pairs in gold proof guise. An additional 68,537 'BU' coins were sold in tubes to other retailers, a further 22,786 were included in the 2016 annual (non-proof) sets and 128 were contained in framed pairs including a larger version of the coin design cast in plaster!

The end of the round pound coin.

The old round pounds are no longer found in circulation, but has that affected their value? The answer is no. In fact, just as I predicted, there is actually less interest in the round pound coins now than there was when it was still possible to find them in circulation. Ultimately they will find their own level and there should (in the long term) be very few, if any, that will be worth more than £1 in normal used condition.

The Check Your Change App is available for Android™ and Apple™ devices

It contains a database of the 700+ different UK decimal coins (in current circulation and the older ones). The app is free to download and use.

Features of the free app:

- Mark coins as owned (including the ability to add a quantity).
- Filter by coins you have or coins you need.
- Running total of coins owned out of the possible total of types.
- The more valuable/sought after coins have a bronze, silver or gold status icon.
- Coins that were only available to purchase are marked clearly, with an icon and can be toggled visible or invisible.
- Mintage figures.
- View large images of the coins.
- Add your own notes to every coin (e.g. condition, where you got it etc).
- The app is free of adverts.

Unlock the premium features (for a small fee) to reveal:

- Valuations for each coin in both 'Used' and 'As New' condition.
- The full range of Strike Your Own Royal Mint packaged coins.

Quantities of each coin can be input and the app will add up the total value of your collection automatically. The valuations within an app can be updated a lot easier than in a printed book and the small fee includes free value updates for one year.

Screenshots showing:

Below left - A main coin summary page with the 50p denomination selected.

Below - A fully enlarged 2017 Isaac Newton 50p £2 image.

The New Twelve-Sided £1 Coin, introduction and specifications

On the 19th March 2014 the Chancellor of the Exchequer announced that a completely new £1 coin would be produced to replace the existing coin. It is hoped that the new coins will be much harder to counterfeit than the single-metal round £1 coins, that were produced from 1983 to 2016 and had become a target for forgers.

The new 12-sided pound first appeared for sale on the 1st January 2017 within the 2017 BU and proof sets. During March 2017 the coins started to appear in circulation, the first were dated 2016 and were closely followed by coins dated 2017. Both 2016 and 2017 coins were made in very large numbers - but despite this, there are still people on eBay trying to claim that the normal 2016 coin is some kind of trial! In a short space of time, a relatively high number of £1 coin varieties and common errors have been observed, including four different types of 'Trial Piece' and also a confirmed fake new £1 coin, too!

Specifications of the new £1 coin:
Diameter (2015 onwards): 23.03mm flat to opposing flat, 23.43mm point to opposing point.
Weight (2015 onwards): 8.75 grammes.
Alloy (2015 onwards): Centre part - Nickel-brass plated in nickel. Outer ring - Nickel brass.
Edge: The edge has alternately milled and plain sections.

2014 - 2016, Royal Mint £1 coin 'TRIAL PIECES'

Trial coins were supplied to vending machine companies for testing and cali-bration purposes. The companies that received them were all obliged under contract to return them by December 31st 2017. Some clearly didn't, as many appeared for sale online quite early on, and continue to do so. These trial coins remain, according to the contract under which they were supplied, the property of the Royal Mint. The legal implications of third party possession of them remains a grey area. Buyer and seller beware!

There are three different vending machine trial £1 coins known (plus a 2014 bi-metallic coin that was probably made in very low numbers and may not have been distributed at all). They all share the same basic reverse design, featuring the Royal Mint crest and 'TRIAL PIECE' below.

Trial Piece
2014 £1 coin
(monometallic)

2014 dated trial coins seem to be the rarest. The main type are made entirely of a brass coloured alloy (i.e. not bi-metallic). They are also a bit smaller and slightly thicker than subsequent coins.

2015 dated trial coins are the most common, they use the same obverse '4th portrait' of the Queen, but are obviously dated 2015 and are all bi-metallic, with a silver coloured inner part and brass coloured outer ring.

There seems to have been extra demand for testing in 2016, as a short run of 2016 dated trials was made. They use exactly the same obverse as the circulation type coin (with 5th portrait of the Queen) and are all bi-metallic.

2014 - 2016, Royal Mint new £1 coin 'TRIAL PIECES' (continued)

Trial Piece 2015 £1 coin

		Used
2014	Bi-metallic with inverted MMXIV edge lettering	? (two seen)
2014 20k?	Very few seen, most were potentially returned	£300 - £400?
2015	Mintage number said to be 234,586*	£30 - £50
2016	Mintage number said to be 1,000*	£100 - £200?

*About 15,000 2015/16 are known to have been returned to the mint, as originally stipulated.

Note: there are known fakes of the trial coins! They are almost certainly from China and omit the micro 'ONE POUND' lettering around the rim of the obverse.

In recent months very few genuine 2014 or 2016 trial coins have been offered for sale.

The 12-sided £1 coin, circulation type

Standard type 2017 £1 coin   Mono-metallic error 2017 £1 coin

The circulation 'new style' £1 coins all feature the same obverse and reverse design. The obverse carries the 5th portrait of the Queen by Jody Clark and features a 'hologram' at the bottom, which depending on the angle it is viewed from, will either show a '£' symbol or a '1'. The reverse, known as the 'Nations of the Crown', is by David Pearce and shows a rose, leek, thistle and shamrock growing from a single stem, set within a crown.

There are a handful of known 2016 mules, which show the main obverse date as 2016 but have been struck in error with a 2017 reverse die, featuring very tiny '2017' dates around the edge.

Concerning the new £1 coins, many other types of errors are known, some of which are quite common. Significant and rarer errors include: coins struck on a single piece of nickel-brass alloy. These coins truly are 'mono-metallic' just like the old round £1 coins. They were first brought to my attention the end of 2017 and I've probably seen about a dozen or more of them since (although only 1x 2016 dated mono-metallic coin so far). In February 2018 the tabloids picked up on them and one that was due to appear in an auction had, according to the auctioneer, been struck on an old round £1 blank in error - I'm sure that isn't true. Having examined the mono-metallic coin shown on the previous page, and due to its weight being almost exactly the same as a normal new £1 coin (the old round pounds were heavier), what I believe has happened is that the mono-metallic coins have been struck on non-pierced outer ring pieces, which is a far more logical explanation and is a known cause of similar error types, e.g. mono-metallic modern £2 coins and also some foreign coin types that should be bi-metallic, but aren't.

Another significant error type seen, which exists for 2016, 2017 and 2018, is also made entirely of gold coloured nickel-brass, but is clearly two separate pieces. Normal coins are actually almost entirely nickel-brass and what appears to have happened with these is that the centre piece has, for whatever reason, not been plated with nickel before eventually being struck as a coin. A few of these are known for 2017 (a lot less it seems for 2016 and 2018). Many people dismiss them as having been entirely plated or messed with in some way. It is a sad state of affairs, there being so many home made 'error' coins on eBay that such activity actually sows the seeds of distrust and any apparent error coin is viewed with much scepticism, even genuine errors.

		Used	BU	Proof
2016	648,936,536	FV		
	Mule, 2017 reverse (with tiny 2017 micro dates around reverse rim)			
		£400 - £600		
	Error, mono-metallic in nickel-brass	Only 1 known		
	With small cross-crosslet mintmark*, sold in packs with a 'last round pound',			
	base metal: £70.00 (9,850 made), in gold: £1995 (new price, max. 100 made)			
	Error, non-plated golden centre piece	no data		
2017	749,616,200 (+80,850 BU versions)	FV	£5.00	£10.00
	Error, mono-metallic nickel-brass	£350 - £400**		
	Error, non-plated golden centre piece	£50 - £150		
	.925 sterling silver proof, 25k max. - £40.00 piedfort proof, ? max. - £75.00			
	.917 gold proof, 2,017 max., price new			£950.00
2018	130,560,000	FV	£5.00	£5.00
2018	Error, non-plated golden centre piece	no data		
2019		FV	£6.00	£6.00
2020	Currently in 2020 sets only		£6.00	£6.00

* The small cross-crosslet mintmark is located above the 'E' of 'ONE' on the silver part, below the crown and looks like this: ☩

** The mono-metallic 2017 £1 coin mentioned above, that was hyped up in the press, sold for £2,375 (£1,900 + commission) at auction on 20/2/18. Others have sold since for £350 - £500 and that kind of value is probably more realistic as a few are known - but anything is only worth what others are prepared to pay!

The 'lefties' and 'righties'!

A variety of note, which is known to affect all current circulation coins, concerns the rim millings (ridges) on the alternate flat sides of the edge. When the coin is held with the Queen up the right way, at the bottom point (below the hologram) most coins have a milled edge on the edge section to the right of the hologram. Some coins, perhaps 1 in 30 or even as low as 1 in 100 (and potentially even lower for the 2017 - 2019 dated coins) have a milled edge section to the left of the hologram.

Regularly encountered errors

Minor raised blob-like areas around and on the Queen and sometimes on raised parts of the reverse seem to be very common and are caused by the dies failing over time.

Dark permanent stains, usually in the form of a ring around the outside of the silver coloured part are very common.

Coins with a raised lip around part of the edge or the entire circumference of the edge are fairly common. This is caused by the coin being struck without the retaining collar properly surrounding it during the moment of impact (the value of such coins tends to be £5 - £10).

Coins that resemble a fried egg with a broken yolk seem very scarce, but have been seen often enough to be of note. This seems to be caused by the centre silver coloured part not being properly lined up (or he brass ring was mis-shapen) within the ring shaped brass coloured part at the point of impact. It usually results in the silver coloured part 'overlapping' and spreading out towards the rim and can sometimes result in a gap between the silver part and the brass part on the opposing side.

Fake New Pound Coins

The first confirmed new-style fake £1 coin was made public on the Check Your Change website in December 2018, after a number were reported to have appeared in change from approximately October to November 2018 onwards.

They are slightly larger than the genuine coin but are also made of two pieces of metal, just like the real ones. They have no micro lettering on either side and the first type (shown below) seem to have a distinct raised flaw going through the 'E' and 'PO' of 'ONE POUND'. Other coins that are very likely to be fakes have been reported recently without the distinct flaw on the reverse. It is thought that these forgeries were made in the UK somewhere. There are some further details on this fake coin and quite a lot of information on error coins on checkyourchange.co.uk.

Fake 2017 £1 coin

What's currently legal tender?

All £2 coins dated from 1986 to date are legal tender. The earlier single metal type coins dated 1986 to 1996 are not often seen in circulation and therefore may not be accepted by some merchants who are unfamiliar with them. All of the single metal type coins tend to be worth a little more than face value, even in used condition. Note that there are fake £2 coins in circulation, mostly with recent commemorative designs. They seem to originate from China.

Which are hard to find?

All of the 1986 to 1996 (single alloy) £2 coins are now hard to find in circulation. The scarcest £2 coin is probably COMMEMORATIVE TYPE 3, the 'Claim of Right' coin, as this was minted in much smaller quantities than the other 1989 £2 coin, and was only issued in Scotland. Some of the more recent £2 coins do sell for more than face value, even in used condition! See listings.

COMMEMORATIVE TYPE 1
A thistle encircled by a laurel wreath, superimposed on St. Andrew's Cross
(1986 Commonwealth Games, Edinburgh)
Reverse design by: Norman Sillman
Edge: XIII COMMONWEALTH GAMES SCOTLAND 1986

1986	8,212,184		Used	As-New	Proof
1986	8,212,184	104,591 Proofs	£3.00	£5.00	£10.00
		Specimen in folder		£10.00	
	58,881	.500 silver UNC	£17.00		
	59,779	.925 sterling silver proof			£22.00
		.917 gold proof			£550.00

COMMEMORATIVE TYPE 2
Intertwined W & M (monogram of William & Mary)
House of Commons Mace, English Crown
TERCENTENARY of the BILL of RIGHTS
1689-1989
Reverse design by: John Lobban
Edge: MILLED

1989	4,432,000		Used	As-New	Proof
1989	4,432,000	84,704 Proofs	£4.00	£6.00	£10.00
		Partially non frosted proof*			£18.00
		Specimen in folder		£12.00	
	25,000	.925 sterling silver proof pair with type 3			£60.00
	10,000	.925 sterling silver piedfort proof pair, with type 3			£65.00

*Proofs that were part of a Bass Charrington promotion appear to have a non frosted bust of the Queen. More comparison is needed at this stage.

COMMEMORATIVE TYPE 3
Intertwined W & M
(monogram of William & Mary)
House of Commons Mace, Scottish Crown
TERCENTENARY of the CLAIM of RIGHT
1689-1989
Reverse design by: John Lobban
Edge: MILLED

			Used	As-New	Proof
1989	346,000	84,704 Proofs	£20.00	£35.00	£35.00
		Specimen in folder		£40.00	
		Specimen folder, including both versions ('Bill' & 'Claim')	£50.00		
	24,852	.925 sterling silver proof pair, with type 2			£60.00
	10,000	.925 sterling silver piedfort proof pair with type 2			£65.00

COMMEMORATIVE TYPE 4
Intertwined W & M
(monogram of William & Mary)
Britannia Seated
BANK of ENGLAND 1694-1994
Reverse design by: Leslie Durbin
Edge: SIC VOS NON VOBIS

☆

			Used	As-New	Proof
1994	1,443,116	67,721 Proofs	£5.00	£10.00	£10.00
		Specimen in folder		£14.00	
	27,957	.925 sterling silver proof			£22.00
	9,569	.925 sterling silver piedfort proof			£30.00
	1,000	.917 gold proof			£650.00
	? Est. 300	Gold proof mule with wrong obverse*			£2200.00

*The obverse of the double sovereign £2 coin was used in error on some of the gold proof issue. As shown above, the head is larger, legend more abbreviated and it omits the words 'TWO POUNDS'.

COMMEMORATIVE TYPE 5
Dove of Peace
(Commemorating 50 years' peace,
since the end of World War II)
Reverse design by: John Mills
Edge: 1945 IN PEACE GOODWILL 1995

			Used	As-New	Proof
1995	5,000,000	60,639 Proofs	£4.00	£9.00	£15.00
		Specimen in folder		£20.00	
	50,000	.925 sterling silver proof			£23.00
	10,000	.925 sterling silver piedfort proof			£25.00
	2,500	.917 gold proof			£600.00

COMMEMORATIVE TYPE 6
UN logo, array of flags
NATIONS UNITED FOR PEACE 1945 - 1995
(50th Anniversary - United Nations)
Reverse design by: Michael Rizzello
Edge: MILLED

			Used	As-New	Proof
1995	1,750,000		£12.00	£18.00	
		Specimen in folder		£22.00	
	175,000	.925 sterling silver proof			£25.00
	10,000	.925 sterling silver piedfort proof			£40.00
	2,098	.917 gold proof			£600.00

COMMEMORATIVE TYPE 7
Football design, with date, 1996, in centre
(10th European Championship)
Reverse design by: John Mills
Edge: TENTH EUROPEAN CHAMPIONSHIP

			Used	As-New	Proof
1996	5,141,350		£8.00	£14.00	£15.00
		Specimen in folder		£20.00	
	50,000	.925 sterling silver proof			£35.00
	10,000	.925 sterling silver piedfort proof			£40.00
	2,098	.917 gold proof (slight varieties exist*)			£600.00

*concerning the type of blank used. Some are flatter, not concave.

BI-METALLIC £2 COINS (1997 onwards)

OBVERSES

OBVERSE 1
(dated 1997 only, but actually issued in 1998)
ELIZABETH II DEI GRA REGINA F D
Elizabeth II, Dei Gratia Regina, Fidei Defensor
(Elizabeth II, By the Grace of God Queen and Defender of the Faith)
Portrait by: Raphael Maklouf

OBVERSE 2
(used 1998 to 2015)
(Also used on commemoratives 8 to 17, 19, 21 and 32)
ELIZABETH II DEI GRATIA REGINA FID DEF
Elizabeth II, Dei Gratia Regina, Fidei Defensor
(Elizabeth II, By the Grace of God Queen and Defender of the Faith)
Portrait by: Ian Rank-Broadley

OBVERSE 2b

OBVERSE 2c

OBVERSE 2d

Variations of obverse 2 - Some of the later reverse designs don't include a date, the face value or both, so these have been incorporated into the obverse legend.

2b: 'TWO POUNDS' at bottom - was used for Commemorative Types 18, 20, 24, 28, 29, 30, 31 & 33
2c: DATE at bottom - was used for Commemorative Types 22, 23 and 25
2d: 'TWO POUNDS' and DATE at bottom - was used for Commemorative Types 26, 27 & 34

OBVERSES (continued)

OBVERSE 3
(used 2015 onwards)
ELIZABETH II DEI GRA REG FID DEF + date
Elizabeth II, Dei Gratia Regina, Fidei Defensor
(Elizabeth II, By the Grace of God Queen and Defender of the Faith)
Portrait by: Jody Clark

OBVERSE 3b

OBVERSE 3c

OBVERSE 3d

OBVERSE 3e

Variations of obverse 3 - Due to the commemorative reverse designs not stating the face value or already featuring the date, there are currently four variations of Obverse 3.

3b: '2 POUNDS' to the left of the Queen - was used for Commemorative Types 33b, 37, 38 and 39.
3c: With no date - was used for Commemorative Type 36.
3d: 'TWO POUNDS' to the left of the Queen, date above - was used for Commemorative Type 34b.
3e: '2 POUNDS' to the left of the Queen, date above - was used for Commemorative Type 41.

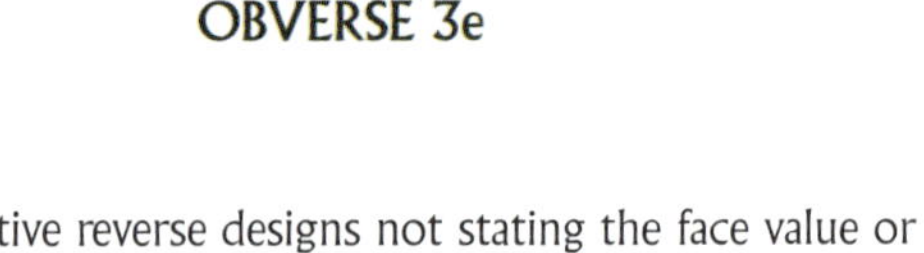

STANDARD (non commemorative) REVERSES:

REVERSE 1 (standard non-commemorative reverse)
(used 1997 to 2015)
Rings, representing stages of development:
from centre, outward: IRON AGE, INDUSTRIAL REVOLUTION
(cogs), ELECTRONIC AGE (silicon chips), INTERNET AGE
Edge: STANDING ON THE SHOULDERS OF GIANTS
Design by: Bruce Rushin

REVERSE 2 (standard non-commemorative reverse)
(used 2015 onwards)
Britannia facing left, holding trident.
Edge: QUATUOR MARIA VINDICO (I claim the four seas)
Design by: Anthony Dufort

TRIAL TYPES
Sailing ship, representing the Mayflower

The 1994 bi-metallic trial £2 coin. Although dated 1994, they were actually released in 1998. The coins were all issued in packs which also contained examples of round nickel-brass (outer) and cupro-nickel (inner) blanks and a nickel-brass ring. The obverse used is a modified OBVERSE 1 - very similar, but the trial obverse has minor differences, for example, a dot instead of a small cross between the 'D' and 'ELIZABETH'.

Edge: DECUS ET TUTAMEN ANNO REGNI XLVI
Value: The bi-metallic pack tends to sell for between £200 and £220.
(loose trial coins are £120 - £140. BEWARE, fakes exist)

Monometallic all-brass £2 trial, dated 1994 and marked 'ROYAL MINT TRIAL' on both sides, also featuring the ship design on the reverse. This particular coin was never made available to the public. They are very rare. **Value £1,000.00 - £2,000.00**

28.40 mm • 12.0 grammes • bi-metal • various edge

DEFINITIVE TYPE 1 (obverse 1, reverse 1)

Year	Mintage		UNC	As-New	Proof
1997	13,734,625		£3.00	£6.00	£7.50
		Specimen in folder		£9.00	
	29,910	.925 silver proof			£20.00
	10,000	.925 silver piedfort proof			£40.00
	2,482	.917 gold proof			£600.00

DEFINITIVE TYPE 2 (obverse 2, reverse 1)

Year	Mintage		UNC	As-New	Proof
1998	91,110,375	100,000 proofs	FV	£6.00	£7.50
1999*	33,719,000	Used: FV	£60.00	£80.00+	
2000	25,770,000		FV	£6.00	£7.50
2001	34,984,750		FV	£6.00	£7.50
2002	13,024,750		FV	£6.00	£7.50
2003	17,531,250		FV	£6.00	£7.50
2004	11,981,500		FV	£6.00	£7.50
2005	3,837,250		FV	£6.00	£7.50
2006	16,715,000		FV	£6.00	£7.50
2007	10,270,000		FV	£6.00	£7.50
2008	30,107,000		FV	£6.00	£7.50
2009	8,775,000		FV	£6.00	£7.50
2010*	6,890,000		FV	£6.00	£7.50
2011	24,375,030		FV	£6.00	£7.50
2012	3,900,000		FV	£6.00	£7.50
2013	15,860,250		FV	£6.00	£7.50
2014	18,200,000		FV	£6.00	£7.50
2015	35,360,058**		FV	£6.00	£7.50

* 1999 was not issued in the proof or BU sets that year and very few people seem to have saved them from change. It is therefore scarce to almost unheard of in top condition. 2010 coins exist with an interesting doubled-die error obverse, most evident on lettering below the queen.

DEFINITIVE TYPE 3 (obverse 3, reverse 2) - The new annual definitive Britannia coin.

Year	Mintage			As-New	Proof
2015	650,000	Used: £3.00		£12.00	£14.00
	15,597	Specimen in folder		£14.00	
	die alignment error **			£20-£50	
		.917 gold proof, price new			£750.00
2016	2,925,000			£10.00	£15.00
		Specimen in folder		£14.00	
		.917 gold proof			£800.00
2017	Unknown	Available in sets only		£10.00	
2018	Unknown	Available in sets only		£10.00	
2019	Unknown	Currently available in sets only	£10.00		

** Many 2015 £2 coins (both types) have been observed with die rotation errors. The 2015 technology coin is also known to exist as a mono-metallic brass alloy coin, struck in error on an unpierced outer ring piece. See the website for a lot more error coin information.

BI-METALLIC COMMEMORATIVE COINS

Note that some Brilliant Uncirculated bi-metallic £2 folders that are still sealed in original plastic wrappers can be worth more than the values shown.

COMMEMORATIVE TYPE 8
Symbolic representation of a stadium with rugby ball and goalposts. '1999' above, 'TWO POUNDS' below
(1999 Rugby World Cup)
Design by: Ron Dutton
Edge: RUGBY WORLD CUP 1999

			UNC	As-New	Proof
1999	4,933,000		£3.00	£7.50	£10.00
		Specimen in folder		£15.00	
	9,665	.925 sterling silver proof			£22.00
	10,000	.925 sterling silver hologram piedfort proof			£60.00
	311	.917 gold proof			£500.00

Noted with incorrect (rotated) die alignment of about 90 degrees.

COMMEMORATIVE TYPE 9
Symbolic representation of Marconi's successful transatlantic wireless transmission of 1901,
'TWO POUNDS' below
Design by: Robert Evans
Edge: WIRELESS BRIDGES THE ATLANTIC...MARCONI 1901...

			UNC	As-New	Proof
2001	4,558,000		£3.00	£7.50	£10.00
		Specimen in folder		£20.00	
	11,488	.925 sterling silver proof			£20.00
	6,759	.925 sterling silver piedfort proof			£30.00
	1,658	.917 gold proof			£550.00

28.40 mm • 12.0 grammes • bi-metal • various edge

a  b 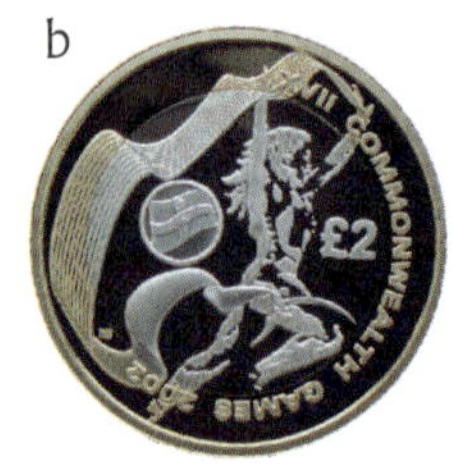 c  d 

COMMEMORATIVE TYPE 10
XVII COMMONWEALTH GAMES 2002
around athlete holding banner, (1 of 4) national flags
(17th Commonwealth Games, Manchester)
Design by: Matthew Bonaccorsi
Edge: SPIRIT OF FRIENDSHIP MANCHESTER 2002

			<u>Used</u>	UNC/As-New	Proof
2002	650,500	10a English flag	£9.00	£20/£30	£35.00
	485,500	10b N. Ireland flag	£27.00	£30/£45	£45.00
	771,750	10c Scottish flag	£7.00	£20/£25	£25.00
	588,500	10d Welsh flag	£10.00	£25/£35	£35.00

The NI coin looks very similar to the England coin. The NI flag has a crowned hand in the centre.

Sets of the 4 Type 10 coins:		
	Specimens in BU card (19,229)	£150.00
	base metal proof set (3,552 felt box. 747 in plastic box)	£180.00
2,553?	.925 sterling silver proof set	£200.00
3,497?	.925 sterling silver piedfort set (coloured flags)	£320.00
315?	.917 gold proof set	no data

COMMEMORATIVE TYPE 11
DNA Double Helix pattern, DNA DOUBLE HELIX,
1953 TWO POUNDS 2003
(50th Anniversary - Discovery of DNA)
Design by: John Mills
Edge: DEOXYRIBONUCLEIC ACID

			UNC	As-New	Proof
2003	4,299,000		£3.00	£7.50	£15.00
	14,105	Specimen in folder		£15.00	
	11,204	.925 sterling silver proof			£30.00
	8,728	.925 sterling silver piedfort proof			£35.00
	1,500	.917 gold proof			£550.00

COMMEMORATIVE TYPE 12

Steam locomotive TWO POUNDS R.TREVITHICK
1804 INVENTION INDUSTRY PROGRESS 2004
(200th anniversary - Steam Locomotive)
Design by: Robert Lowe
Edge: pattern of arcs & curves, representing viaducts

			UNC	As-New	Proof
2004	5,004,500		£3.00	£7.50	£15.00
	14,447	Specimen in folder		£16.00	
	1,923 max.	.925 sterling silver BU version in pack			£40.00?
	10,233 of 25k	.925 sterling silver proof			£35.00
	5,303 of 10k	.925 sterling silver piedfort cased proof			£50.00
	1,500	.917 gold proof			£550.00

COMMEMORATIVE TYPE 13

Swords, Maces, Croziers in a star-burst pattern,
1605-2005, TWO POUNDS
(400th anniversary - Gunpowder Plot)
Design by: Peter Forster
Edge: REMEMBER REMEMBER THE FIFTH OF NOVEMBER*

			UNC	As-New	Proof
2005	5,140,500		£3.00	£7.50	£15.00
	12,044	Specimen in folder		£30.00	
	4,394	.925 sterling silver proof			£25.00
	4,584	.925 sterling silver piedfort proof			£55.00
	914	.917 gold proof			£550.00

* These very often end up having missing tails on the 'R's of the edge lettering, so that they can in extreme cases read PEMEMBEP PEMEMBEP THE FIFTH OF NOVEMBEP. This problem with certain edge letters has also been noted on some other £2 and £1 coins. It makes them a little more interesting, but it is my opinion that such errors should have no real influence on the value. I say should have no real influence on the value, but it seems it can sometimes have an affect on value, at least on eBay, where PEMEMBER coins in normal used condition were once exchanging hands for £10 and examples in UNC or near to UNC condition have been sold in the past for £20 - £30. Judging by the number of them that is constantly available, they should theoretically attract no premium.

> ## INFO
>
> Some £2 coins still sealed in original 'specimen' BU packaging have been known to sell for considerably more than shown.

28.40 mm • 12.0 grammes • bi-metal • various edge

COMMEMORATIVE TYPE 14

St. Paul's Cathedral, floodlit with spotlights.
1945-2005, TWO POUNDS
(60th anniversary - End of World War II)
Design by: Robert Elderton
Edge: IN VICTORY: MAGNANIMITY, IN PEACE: GOODWILL

			UNC	As-New	Proof
2005	10,191,000		£3.00	£7.50	
	13,904	(folder including special medallion)		£25.00	
	21,734	.925 sterling silver proof			£30.00
	Not Known	*Error edge: REMEMBER REMEMBER THE FIFTH OF			
		NOVEMBER .925 silver proof			£400.00?
	4,798	.925 sterling silver piedfort proof			£45.00
	2,924	.917 gold proof			no data

Noted with slightly incorrect (rotated) die alignment.

* The edge error 60th Anniversary of the End of WWII £2 coin incorrectly has the edge inscription of the other themed £2 coin struck that year to commemorate the gunpowder plot.

COMMEMORATIVE TYPE 15

Portrait of Isambard Kingdom Brunel in front of machinery
TWO POUNDS | 2006
(200th anniversary - Birth of Isambard Kingdom Brunel)
Design by: Rod Kelly
Edge: 1806-59 . ISAMBARD KINGDOM BRUNEL . ENGINEER

			UNC	As-New	Proof
2006	7,928,250		£3.00	£7.50	£15.00
	10,941	Specimens in folder (with Type 16)		£24.00	
	7,251 of 20k	.925 sterling silver proof			£30.00
	3,199 of 5k	.925 sterling silver piedfort proof			£50.00
	1,071 of 1,500	.917 gold proof			£550.00

Known to exist with its outer ring made from a 2006 heroic acts 50p! Believed unique.

The words 'TWO POUNDS' above Mr Brunel on the reverse often looks more like 'TWO DOUNDS', due to the tail of the 'P' being obscured by the join between the inner and outer metal types.

The Brunel coins (types 15 and 16) were also sold in pairs in a folder and also cased as silver proofs.

COMMEMORATIVE TYPE 16

Representation of the engineering achievements of I.K.Brunel,
2006 | BRUNEL | TWO POUNDS
(200th anniversary - Birth of Isambard Kingdom Brunel)
Design by: Robert Evans
Edge: SO MANY IRONS IN THE FIRE

			UNC	As-New	Proof
2006	7,452,250		£3.00	£7.50	£15.00
	10,941	Specimens in folder (with Type 15)	£24.00		
	5,375 of 20k	.925 sterling silver proof			£40.00
	Not Known	.925 sterling silver proof with no edge lettering			£300.00?
	3,018 of 5k	.925 sterling silver piedfort proof			£50.00
	746 of 1,500	.917 gold proof*			£550.00

* Noted with certificate no. 1054, which shouldn't be possible! Printing mix up with Type 15?

COMMEMORATIVE TYPE 17

Jigsaw pieces of the English rose and Scottish thistle,
TWO | 2007 | POUNDS | 1707
(300th anniversary - Act of Union between England and Scotland)
Design by: Yvonne Holton
Edge: UNITED INTO ONE KINGDOM

			UNC	As-New	Proof
2007	7,545,000		£3.00	£7.50	£15.00
	8,863	Specimen in folder	£20.00		
	8,310	.925 sterling silver proof			£20.00
	4,000	.925 sterling silver piedfort proof			£50.00
	750	.917 gold proof			£550.00

COMMEMORATIVE TYPE 18 (A & B)

Five link chain with broken link as the nought in 1807,
AN ACT FOR THE ABOLITION OF THE SLAVE TRADE | 2007
(200th anniversary - Abolition of the British slave trade)
Design by: David Gentleman
Edge: AM I NOT A MAN AND A BROTHER
Obverse: 2b

				UNC	As-New	Proof
2007	B	8,445,000	(no 'DG' initials)	£7.50	Hard to find	
	A	8,688	Specimen in folder ('DG' to right of chain)	£25.00		£20.00
	A	7,095	.925 sterling silver proof ('DG' to right of chain)			£25.00*
	A	3,990	.925 sterling silver piedfort proof			£55.00
	A	1,000 max	.917 gold proof			£550.00

Type A has 'DG' initials to the right of the '1807'. Type B has no initials and a textured background.
A silver proof version of this coin is known to exist with the 'THE 4TH OLYMPIAD LONDON'
edge legend, obviously meant for Type 19. See also the note under Type 14.

99

28.40 mm • 12.0 grammes • bi-metal • various edge

COMMEMORATIVE TYPE 19
Running Track
LONDON OLYMPIC CENTENARY | 1908 | TWO POUNDS | 2008
(Centenary - 1908 London Olympics)
Design by: Thomas T Docherty
Edge: THE 4TH OLYMPIAD LONDON
Obverse: 2

			Used	As-New	Proof
2008	910,000		£4.00	£20.00	£20.00
	14,426 of 100k	Specimen in folder		£40.00	
	6,841 of 20k	.925 sterling silver proof			£40.00
	1,619 of 2,000	.925 sterling silver piedfort proof			£75.00
	1,908	.917 gold proof			£500.00

COMMEMORATIVE TYPE 20
Olympic flag and two hands
BEIJING 2008 | LONDON 2012
(Olympic handover ceremony)
Design by: Royal Mint in House
Edge: I CALL UPON THE YOUTH OF THE WORLD
Obverse: 2b

			Used	As-New	Proof
2008	918,000		£4.00	£20.00	
	57,346 of 250k	Specimen in folder		£40.00	
	30,000	.925 sterling silver proof			£30.00
	3,000	.925 sterling silver piedfort proof			£65.00
	3,250	.917 gold proof			£550.00

COMMEMORATIVE TYPE 21
Darwin facing ape
1809 DARWIN 2009 | TWO POUNDS
(200th anniversary - birth of Charles Darwin)
Design by: Suzie Zamit
Edge: ON THE ORIGIN OF SPECIES 1859
Obverse: 2

			UNC	As-New	Proof
2009	3,903,000		£3.00	£7.50	£10.00
	18,658 of 25k	Specimen in folder		£25.00	
	9,357	.925 sterling silver proof			£65.00
	3,282	.925 sterling silver piedfort proof			£80.00
	1,000	.917 gold proof			£550.00

28.40 mm • 12.0 grammes • bi-metal • various edge

COMMEMORATIVE TYPE 22

Burns quote
1759 ROBERT BURNS 1796 | TWO POUNDS
(250 years anniversary - birth of Robert Burns)
Design by: Royal Mint in House
Edge: SHOULD AULD ACQUAINTANCE BE FORGOT
Obverse: 2c

			UNC	As-New	Proof
2009	3,253,000		£3.00	£8.00	£15.00
	23,455	Specimen in folder		£20.00	
	9,188	.925 sterling silver proof			£50.00
	3,500	.925 sterling silver piedfort proof			£80.00
	1,000	.917 gold proof			no data

COMMEMORATIVE TYPE 23

Nurses hands feeling for a pulse
1820 - FLORENCE NIGHTINGALE - 1910 | TWO POUNDS
(150 years of modern nursing and to the centenary of the
death of Florence Nightingale)
Design by: Gordon Summers
Edge: 150 YEARS OF NURSING
Obverse: 2c

			UNC	As-New	Proof
2010	6,175,000		£3.00	£10.00	£10.00
	14,905 of 25k	Specimen in folder		£40.00	
	5,117 of 20k	.925 sterling silver proof			£60.00
	2,770 of 3,5k	.925 sterling silver piedfort proof			no data
	472 of 1,000	.917 gold proof			no data

An error struck on a nickel plated steel blank is known to exist - it is thought to be a blank
intended for a Gambian 50 Butots (the Royal Mint also strike coins for many other countries).

COMMEMORATIVE TYPE 24

King James' Bible
KING JAMES BIBLE | 1611 - 2011
(400 years anniversary - King James' Bible)
Design by: Paul Stafford & Benjamin Wright
Edge: THE AUTHORISED VERSION
Obverse: 2b

			Used	As-New	Proof
2011	975,000		£4.00	£30.00	£30.00
	11,317 of 25k	Specimen in folder		£55.00	
	4,494 of 20k	.925 sterling silver proof			£50.00
	2,394 of 3,5k	.925 sterling silver piedfort proof			£80.00
	355 of 1000	.917 gold proof			no data

28.40 mm • 12.0 grammes • bi-metal • various edge

COMMEMORATIVE TYPE 25
Mary Rose
THE MARY ROSE | TWO POUNDS
(500 Years - Mary Rose)
Design by: John Bergdahl
Edge: 1511 . YOUR NOBLEST SHIPPE .
Obverse: 2c

			Used	As-New	Proof
2011	1,040,000		£4.00	£30.00	£25.00
	8,277 of 25k	Specimen in folder		£50.00	
	6,618 of 20k	.925 sterling silver proof			£70.00
	2,680 of ?2k	.925 sterling silver piedfort proof			£90.00
	692 of 1000	.917 gold proof			£800.00

COMMEMORATIVE TYPE 26
Olympic Handover
LONDON 2012 | RIO 2016
(Olympic handover ceremony)
Design by: Jonathan Olliffe
Edge: I CALL UPON THE YOUTH OF THE WORLD
Obverse: 2d

			Used	As-New	Proof
2012	845,000		£4.00	£20.00	
	18,275	Specimen in folder		£50.00	
	3,781 of ?12k	.925 sterling silver proof			£50.00
	2000 sold	.925 sterling silver piedfort proof			£80.00
	771 of 100 max	.917 gold proof			£900.00

COMMEMORATIVE TYPE 27
Charles Dickens
1812 CHARLES DICKENS 1870
(200th anniversary - birth of Charles Dickens)
Design by: Matthew Dent
Edge: SOMETHING WILL TURN UP
Obverse: 2d

			UNC	As-New	Proof
2012	8,190,000		£3.00	£7.50	£14.00
	15,035*	Specimen in folder		£40.00	
	2,631 of 20k	.925 sterling silver proof			£50.00
	1279 of 2000	.925 sterling silver piedfort proof			£70.00
	202 of 850	.917 gold proof, price new			£900.00

*Plus 7,726 in packages combining stamps with the coin.

COMMEMORATIVE TYPE 28
Underground Roundal
1863 | UNDERGROUND | 2013
(150th anniversary - The London Underground)
Design by: Edwina Ellis
Edge: MIND THE GAP
Obverse: 2b

		Used	As-New	Proof
2013	1,560,000	£3.00	£15.00	£15.00
	11,647 pairs of coins* Type 28 and 29 Specimens in folder £25.00			
	1,185 of 7.5k	.925 sterling silver proof		£60.00
	162 of 2.5k	.925 sterling silver piedfort proof		£90.00
	21 of 750	.917 gold proof, price new (111 also sold in pairs)		£750.00

* Plus another 9,250 pairs of Underground coins combined with stamps.

Errors: Noted completely in brass, struck on an un-pierced outer ring. Also seen with incorrect patterned edge design of Type 29.

COMMEMORATIVE TYPE 29
Underground Train
1863 | LONDON UNDERGROUND | 2013
(150th anniversary - The London Underground)
Design by: Edward Barber and Jay Osgerby
Edge: A pattern of circles connected by lines.
Obverse: 2b

		Used	As-New	Proof
2013	1,690,000	£3.00	£15.00	£15.00
	2,042 of 7.5k	.925 sterling silver proof*		£50.00
	186 of 2.5k	.925 sterling silver piedfort proof		£90.00
	29 of 750	.917 gold proof, price new (111 also sold in pairs)		£750.00

* A further 2,204 silver proof pairs of both Underground coins were sold : £90
Piedfort proof pair of both Underground coins : £150.00

COMMEMORATIVE TYPE 30
Spade Guinea
ANNIVERSARY OF THE GOLDEN GUINEA | 2013
(350th anniversary - the Guinea)
Design by: Anthony Smith
Edge: WHAT IS A GUINEA? 'TIS A SPLENDID THING
Obverse: 2b

		UNC	As-New	Proof
2013	2,990,000	£3.00	£16.00	£25.00
	10,340	Specimen in folder	£40.00	
	1640 of 12k	.925 sterling silver proof		£80.00
	969 of 4,013	.925 sterling silver piedfort proof		£100.00
	284 of 1100	.917 gold proof		no data

28.40 mm • 12.0 grammes • bi-metal • various edge

COMMEMORATIVE TYPE 31

Design from Kitchener recruitment poster
THE FIRST WORLD WAR 1914 - 1918 | 2014
(Centenary - Start of WWI)
Design by: John Bergdahl
Edge: THE LAMPS ARE GOING OUT ALL OVER EUROPE
Obverse: 2b

			UNC	As-New	Proof
2014	5,720,000		£3.00	£10.00	£15.00
	40,357	Specimen in folder*		£20.00	
	4,983 of 8,014	.925 sterling silver proof			£60.00
	2,496 of 4,514	.925 sterling silver piedfort proof			£80.00
	734 of 825	.917 gold proof			£900.00

*10,490 were also combined with stamps. **Errors:** One with outer ring made from a 2014 standard 50p. Two seen completely in brass and a single mule has been seen with incorrect Obv 2, instead of 2b (i.e. missing 'TWO POUNDS').

COMMEMORATIVE TYPE 32

Top of a Lighthouse
1514 TRINITY HOUSE 2014 | TWO POUNDS
(500 years of Trinity house)
Design by: Joe Whitlock Blundell and David Eccles
Edge: SERVING THE MARINER
Obverse 2

			UNC	As-New	Proof
2014	3,705,000		£3.00	£10.00	£20.00
	10,521	Specimen in folder, price new		£20.00	
	1,285 of 4,717	.925 sterling silver proof, price new			£50.00
	652 of 3,514	.925 sterling silver piedfort proof, price new			£100.00
	204 of 375	.917 gold proof			£900.00

COMMEMORATIVE TYPE 33a

Royal Navy Battleship
THE FIRST WORLD WAR 1914 - 1918 | 2015
(Centenary - WWI, Royal Navy themed coin)
Design by: David Rowlands
Edge: THE SURE SHIELD OF BRITAIN
With Obverse type 2b, shown to right

			As-New	Proof
2015	39,009	Not circulated, sets/packages only		Proof from set: £20.00
		Specimen in folder	£15.00	
	8,500 max	.925 sterling silver proof, price new		£60.00
	4,000 max	.925 sterling silver piedfort proof, price new		£100.00
	900 max	.917 gold proof		£800.00

COMMEMORATIVE TYPE 33b
Royal Navy Battleship
THE FIRST WORLD WAR 1914 - 1918 | 2015
(Centenary - WWI, Royal Navy themed coin)
Design by: David Rowlands
Edge: THE SURE SHIELD OF BRITAIN
With Obverse type 3b, shown to right

	Used	As-New*
2015		
650,000	£4.00	£15.00?

* Hard to find in very high grade as this coins is a circulation type only. Noted with incorrect (rotated) die alignment. Also of note are the 'flag' and 'cat on mast' types, which are colloquial terms for extra features at the top of the mast, both of which have been caused by die damage.

COMMEMORATIVE TYPE 34a
King John with bishop and a baron
MAGNA CARTA | 1215 - 2015
(King John signing the Magna Carta)
Design by: John Bergdahl
Edge: FOUNDATION OF LIBERTY
With Obverse type 2d, shown to right

		As-New	Proof
2015	32,818	Not circulated, sets/packages only	Proof from set: £25.00
		Specimen in folder	£17.00
	1500	.925 sterling silver proof, in sets only*	£75.00?

*This silver proof coin appears to have been made for silver proof sets only, which contain the 5 main commemorative coins of 2015. The main silver proof Magna Carta coins are all Type 34b.

COMMEMORATIVE TYPE 34b
King John with bishop and a baron
MAGNA CARTA | 1215 - 2015
(King John signing the Magna Carta)
Design by: John Bergdahl
Edge: FOUNDATION OF LIBERTY
Obverse type 3d, shown to right

		Used	As-New*	Proof
2015	1,495,000	£3.00	£10.00?	
	4000 max	.925 sterling silver proof		£70.00
	2000 max	.925 sterling silver piedfort proof		£100.00
	400 max	.917 gold proof		£800.00

* Hard to find in perfect condition due to the poor standard of current circulation coins.

105

The 2015 Commemorative £2 coins on the previous pages lack continuity and can be confusing. For each of the two coins (First World War Navy and Magna Carta) two different obverses were used during the year, one with the 4th portrait of the Queen and the other with the new 5th portrait. There are therefore four basic designs. The whole thing is further complicated by the proof issues, which for the Navy coin all use the 4th portrait and for the Magna Carta coin, use the 5th portrait, except for the base metal proof coin (from sets) which features the 4th portrait and early versions of the Magna Carta silver proof coins which were sold in sets of 2015 commemorative coins and feature the 4th portrait.

COMMEMORATIVE TYPE 35
Stylised representation of 'Pals Battalion'
THE FIRST WORLD WAR 1914 - 1918 | 2016
(Centenary - WWI, Army themed coin)
Design by: Tim Sharp of the creative agency Uniform
Edge: FOR KING AND COUNTRY
Obverse 3b

		UNC	As-New	Proof
2016	9,550,000	£5.00	£10.00	£16.00
19,066	Specimen in folder, price new		£15.00	
1,703 of 5k	.925 sterling silver proof			£60.00
931 of 2,500	.925 sterling silver piedfort proof			£70.00
279 of 750	.917 gold proof, price new			£825.00

COMMEMORATIVE TYPE 36
Scene from the Great Fire of London
1666 THE GREAT FIRE OF LONDON 2016 | TWO POUNDS
(350th Anniversary of the Great Fire of London)
Design by: Aaron West
Edge: THE WHOLE CITY IN DREADFUL FLAMES
Obverse 3c

		UNC	As-New	Proof
2016	1,625,000	£3.00	£14.00	£16.00
23,215*	Specimen in folder		£15.00	
1,649 of 7,5k	.925 sterling silver proof			£65.00
1,356 of 3,500	.925 sterling silver piedfort proof, price new			£110.00
259 of 800	.917 gold proof, price new			£825.00

* 4,857 sold in tubes to other retailers.

Types 35 & 36 have been seen completely in brass without the inner silver coloured part (a mint error). Both were contained within BU sets.

106

COMMEMORATIVE TYPE 37
Marotte and Jester's hat
WILLIAM SHAKESPEARE | 2016
(300th Anniversary of Shakespeare's death. Comedy theme)
Design by: John Bergdahl
Edge: ALL THE WORLDS A STAGE (in italic on proofs?)
Obverse 3b

			UNC	As-New	Proof
2016	4,355,000		£3.00	£14.00	£19.00
	22,060 each	*The 3 Shakespeare coins in folder	£28.00		
	951 of 5k	.925 sterling silver proof			£65.00
	533 of 2,500	.925 sterling silver piedfort proof			£80.00
	152 of 300?	.917 gold proof, price new			£825.00

COMMEMORATIVE TYPE 38
Crown and Sword
WILLIAM SHAKESPEARE | 2016
(300th Anniversary of Shakespeare's death. History theme)
Design by: John Bergdahl
Edge: THE HOLLOW CROWN (in italic on proofs?)
Obverse 3b

			UNC	As-New	Proof
2016	5,655,000		£3.00	£14.00	£19.00
	965 of 5k	.925 sterling silver proof			£65.00
	624 of 2,500	.925 sterling silver piedfort proof, price new			£110.00
	156 of 300?	.917 gold proof, price new			£825.00

COMMEMORATIVE TYPE 39
Skull and Rose
WILLIAM SHAKESPEARE | 2016
(300th Anniversary of Shakespeare's death. Tragedy theme)
Design by: John Bergdahl
Edge: WHAT A PIECE OF WORK IS A MAN
(in italic script on proofs)
Obverse 3b

			UNC	As-New	Proof
2016	4,615,000		£3.00	£14.00	£19.00
	1,004 of 5k	.925 sterling silver proof			£65.00
	679 of 2,500	.925 sterling silver piedfort proof, price new			£110.00
	209 of 300	.917 gold proof, price new			£825.00

* These 3 coins in "Brilliant Uncirculated" form were only sold together. In addition to that, 3,500 'comedy', 6,341 'history' and 6,550 'tragedy' coins were sold in tubes to other retailers. Other higher denomination and precious metal Shakespeare themed coins were also sold.

107

28.40 mm • 12.0 grammes • bi-metal • various edge

COMMEMORATIVE TYPE 40
Jane Austen Silhouette and signature
JANE AUSTEN 1817 - 2017 | TWO POUNDS
(200th Anniversary of Jane Austen's death)
Design by: Dominique Evans
Edge: THERE IS NO DOING WITHOUT MONEY
Obverse 3

			As-New	Proof
2017	54,729	Available in sets/packs only	£25.00	
8,000 max.		.925 sterling silver proof		£90.00
4,000 max.		.925 sterling silver piedfort proof		£90.00
884 max.		.917 gold proof		£700.00

COMMEMORATIVE TYPE 41
Biplane from above
1914 - 1918 | THE WAR IN THE AIR
(Centenary - WWI, Aviation themed coin)
Design by: tangerine (design agency)
Edge: THE SKY RAINED HEROES
Obverse 3e

			As-New	Proof
2017	47,703	Available in sets/packs only	£13.00	
7,000 max.		.925 sterling silver proof		£60.00
3,500 max.		.925 sterling silver Piedfort proof		£80.00
634 max.		.917 gold proof, price new		£840.00

COMMEMORATIVE TYPE 42
'FRANKENSTEIN' in a style reminiscent of an ECG
Above: BICENTENARY OF MARY SHELLEY'S
Below: 1818 THE MODERN PROMETHEUS 2018
(200th Anniversary of Mary Shelley's Frankenstein novel)
Design by: Thomas T. Docherty
Edge: A SPARK OF BEING
Obverse 3b

		As-New	Proof
2018	Available in sets/packs only	£10.00	£15.00
4,500 max	.925 sterling silver proof, price new		£67.50
1,818 max	.925 sterling silver Piedfort proof, price new		£110.00
400 max	.917 gold proof, price new		£845.00

COMMEMORATIVE TYPE 43
Badge of the Royal Air Force
THE 100th ANNIVERSARY OF THE ROYAL AIR FORCE |
1918 - 2018
(Centenary - The establishment of the Royal Air Force, 1 of 5)
Design by: Rhys Morgan
Edge: PER ARDUA AD ASTRA
Obverse 3b

		As-New	Proof
2018	Available in sets / packs only	£10.00	£15.00
7,500 max	.925 sterling silver proof, price new		£67.50
3,000 max	.925 sterling silver Piedfort proof, price new		£110.00
1,000 max	.917 gold proof, price new		£845.00

COMMEMORATIVE TYPE 44
Stylised 'THE TRUTH UNTOLD THE PITY OF WAR'
THE FIRST WORLD WAR - ARMISTICE - 1918 |
TWO POUNDS
(Centenary - WWI, Armistice themed coin)
Design by: Stephen Raw
Edge: WILFRED OWEN KILLED IN ACTION 4 NOV 1918
Obverse 3

		As-New	Proof
2018	Available in sets / packs only	£10.00	£15.00
7,500 max	.925 sterling silver proof, price new		£67.50
2,500 max	.925 sterling silver Piedfort proof, price new		£110.00
750 max	.917 gold proof, price new		£845.00

Seen with incorrect die alignment (approx. 80 degrees out) contained within a BU set.
Other precious metal higher value Armistice themed coins, with different designs, were also sold.

COMMEMORATIVE TYPE 45
Spitfire
SPITFIRE RAF | 1918 - 2018
(Centenary - The establishment of the Royal Air Force, 2 of 5)
Design by: Richard Talbot & Neil Talbot
Edge: PER ARDUA AD ASTRA
Obverse 3b

		As-New	Proof
2018	Available in sets / packs only	£10.00	£15.00
	.925 sterling silver proof, price new		TBC
	.925 sterling silver Piedfort proof, price new		TBC
	.917 gold proof, price new		TBC

28.40 mm • 12.0 grammes • bi-metal • various edge

COMMEMORATIVE TYPE 46
Vulcan
RAF 1918 - 2018 | VULCAN
(Centenary - The establishment of the Royal Air Force, 3 of 5)
Design by: Richard Talbot & Neil Talbot
Edge: PER ARDUA AD ASTRA
Obverse 3b

		As-New	Proof
2018	Available in sets/packs only	£10.00	£15.00
7,500 max	.925 sterling silver proof, price new		£67.50
3,000 max	.925 sterling silver Piedfort proof, price new		£110.00
1,000 max	.917 gold proof, price new		£845.00

COMMEMORATIVE TYPE 47
Captain James Cook (1)
1768 - 2018 | CAPTAIN JAMES COOK | 250
(To commemorate the HM Bark Endeavour voyage, 1 of 3)
Design by: Gary Breeze
Edge: OCEANI INVESTIGATOR ACERRIMVS
Obverse 3b

		As-New	Proof
2018	Available in sets/packs only	£10.00	£15.00
4,795 max	.925 sterling silver proof, price new		£67.50
340 max	.917 gold proof, price new		£845.00

COMMEMORATIVE TYPE 48
Sea King
SEA KING | RAF 1918 - 2018
(Centenary - The establishment of the Royal Air Force, 4 of 5)
Design by: Richard Talbot & Neil Talbot
Edge: PER ARDUA AD ASTRA
Obverse 3b

		As-New	Proof
2018	Available in sets/packs only	£10.00	£15.00
7,500 max	.925 sterling silver proof, price new		£67.50
3,000 max	.925 sterling silver Piedfort proof, price new		£110.00
1,000 max	.917 gold proof, price new		£845.00

COMMEMORATIVE TYPE 49
Lightning II
RAF 1918 - 2018 | LIGHTNING II
(Centenary - The establishment of the Royal Air Force, 5 of 5)
Design by: Richard Talbot & Neil Talbot
Edge: PER ARDUA AD ASTRA
Obverse 3b

		As-New	Proof
2018	Available in sets/packs only	£10.00	£15.00
7,500 max	.925 sterling silver proof, price new		£67.50
3,000 max	.925 sterling silver Piedfort proof, price new		£110.00
1,000 max	.917 gold proof, price new		£845.00

COMMEMORATIVE TYPE 50
75th Anniversary of D-Day
D-DAY 75TH ANNIVERSARY | 2019
(To mark the 75th Anniversary of the Normandy landings)
Design by: Stephen Taylor
Edge: THE LONGEST DAY
Obverse 3b

		As-New	Proof
2019	Available in sets/packs only	£10.00	£15.00
5,000 max	.925 sterling silver proof, price new		£67.50
2,000 max	.925 sterling silver Piedfort proof, price new		£110.00
400 max	.917 gold proof, price new		£1,020.00

Also available as silver and gold proofs accompanied by old newspapers.

COMMEMORATIVE TYPE 51
Wedgwood
WEDGWOOD | 1759 - 2019
(260 years since the establishment of Wedgwood)
Design by: Wedgwood Design Team
Edge: EVERYTHING GIVES WAY TO EXPERIMENT
Obverse 3b

		As-New	Proof
2019	Available in sets/packs only	£10.00	£15.00
3,000 max	.925 sterling silver proof, price new		£67.50
1,250 max	.925 sterling silver Piedfort proof, price new		£110.00
225 max	.917 gold proof, price new		£1,055.00

28.40 mm • 12.0 grammes • bi-metal • various edge

COMMEMORATIVE TYPE 52
Samuel Pepys
SAMUEL PEPYS DIARIST | 1669 - 2019
(To mark 350 years since the last diary entry by Samuel Pepys)
Design by: Gary Breeze
Edge: THE GOOD GOD PREPARE ME
Obverse 3b

		As-New	Proof
2019	Available in sets/packs only	£10.00	£15.00
2,500 max	.925 sterling silver proof, price new		£67.50
1,019 max	.925 sterling silver Piedfort proof, price new		£110.00
225 max	.917 gold proof, price new		£1,055.00

COMMEMORATIVE TYPE 53
Captain James Cook (2)
1768 - 2018 | CAPTAIN JAMES COOK | 250
(To commemorate the HM Bark Endeavour voyage, 2 of 3)
Design by: Gary Breeze
Edge: OCEANI INVESTIGATOR ACERRIMVS?
Obverse 3b

		As-New	Proof
2019	Available in sets/packs only	£10.00	
4,795 max	.925 sterling silver proof, price new		£67.50
?	.925 sterling silver Piedfort proof, price new		?
340 max	.917 gold proof, price new		£1,055.00

Doesn't seem to have been made available in silver piedfort guise.

COMMEMORATIVE TYPE 54
Agatha Christie
100 YEARS OF MYSTERY | 1920 | (signature) | 2020
(100 years since the publication of Agatha Christie's first novel)
Design by: David Lawrence
Edge: LITTLE GREY CELLS
Obverse 3b

		As-New	Proof
2020	Most likely to be available in sets/packs only	£10.00	TBC
	.925 sterling silver proof, price new		TBC
	.925 sterling silver Piedfort proof, price new		TBC
	.917 gold proof, price new		TBC

COMMEMORATIVE TYPE 55
VE-Day 75th Anniversary
1945 - 2020 | VICTORY IN EUROPE DAY
(To mark the 75th Anniversary of VE-Day)
Design by: Dominique Evans
Edge: JUST TRIUMPH AND PROUD SORROW
Obverse 3b

		As-New	Proof
2020	Most likely to be available in sets/packs only	£10.00	
4,750 max	.925 sterling silver proof, price new		£67.50
1,635 max	.925 sterling silver Piedfort proof, price new		£110.00
475 max	.917 gold proof, price new		£1,055.00

Also made available various postal numismatic covers.

COMMEMORATIVE TYPE 56
Mayflower Commemorative
1620 | 2020 | MAYFLOWER
(400 Years since the voyage of the Mayflower)
Design by: Chris Costello
Edge: UNDERTAKEN FOR THE GLORY OF GOD
Obverse 3b

		As-New	Proof
2020	Most likely to be available in sets/packs only	£10.00	TBC
	.925 sterling silver proof, price new		TBC
	.925 sterling silver Piedfort proof, price new		TBC
	.917 gold proof, price new		TBC

COMMEMORATIVE TYPE 57
Captain James Cook (3)
1768 - 2018 | CAPTAIN JAMES COOK | 250
(To commemorate the HM Bark Endeavour voyage, 3 of 3)
Design by: Gary Breeze
Edge: OCEANI INVESTIGATOR ACERRIMVS?
Obverse 3b

		As-New	Proof
2020	Available in sets/packs only	£10.00?	
	.925 sterling silver proof, price new		TBC
	.925 sterling silver Piedfort proof, price new		TBC
	.917 gold proof, price new		TBC

What's currently legal tender?

All £5 coins are technically legal tender but are not widely accepted in shops as people are simply not familiar with them.

Look out for non UK £5 coins being offered for face value as these are often from smaller provinces/islands and are therefore not legal tender in the United Kingdom (and often aren't legal tender in the province stated on them either). Particularly worrying are the coins from Tristan da Cunha, a tiny island group with a population of less than 300. So-called £5 coins from Tristan da Cunha often look very British but simply have 'TDC' in the legend. Also, earlier crown coins should not be confused with these post-1990 £5 crowns. The crowns struck from 1972 to 1981 have a face value of 25p.

Which are hard to find?

All of these large coins are hard to find in circulation because they tend to get hoarded by the public when they are new and they are also made in lower numbers than the other, more widely used denominations. They are also heavy and not really practical to carry around for day-to-day transactions.

Recently released mintage figures reveal that many of the newest coins (that were never made available at £5 face value in post offices, like they used to be) were struck in fairly low numbers. This is simply because when they were new and sold in packs, there wasn't much demand for them. The recent obsession with mintage numbers and the publication of the figures instantly created more demand for them, resulting in a few that have risen in value over the last year or so. Remember these are coins that were fairly unpopular when new; it is only the publication of mintage numbers and basically a little social media/eBay frenzy that has caused them to go up in value now. In the future they may end up being just as unpopular as they were when they were sold new!

Reorganisation in this book

The Royal Mint have increased the output of different £5 crown coins they produce substantially over the years. It used to be (way back) a special coin for coronations and jubilees, something struck every few years. They diversified to include other occasions related to senior royals, such as weddings, birthdays, anniversaries etc, but in recent years they've gone a bit mad and are churning out £5 coins at an alarming rate! During the entire 100 year period 1900-1999 there were 27 crowns issued. In 2017 alone, there were 19!

The whole thing has been complicated further by the issuance of silver-proof-only coins in a number of different themed series and the production of cu-ni coins based on the designs of what were originally considered to be silver/gold bullion issues. I'm not sure if many people really care much either; In comparison to lower denominations I hear of very little demand for £5 coins on the grapevine; most people seem to prefer to collect the lower denominations that can be found in change. Recent £5 coin issues seem to lack any kind of structure, have no real direction and while there are some hardcore collectors of them, I feel many people have been put off.

In an attempt to put it all in some kind of order I have decided to split the FIVE POUNDS section into two parts. Perhaps it's not ideal and I'm not entirely satisfied with it, but let's see how this goes...

FIVE POUNDS Pt.1 contains all pre 2009 coins plus any newer coins that commemorate Royal events or are available in humble base metal form at a cost of less than £15.00 when bought new.

FIVE POUNDS Pt.2 contains the post 2008 silver-proof only coins that don't have a royal theme plus special sets of £5 coins and any derived oddities like the bullion based Queen's beast series of cu-ni £5 coins that I also feel don't belong within the main £5 crowns section.

COMMEMORATIVE TYPE 1
Standard portrait of QE II
Design by: Raphael Maklouf
Double "E" monogram, crowned
Design by: Leslie Durbin

			Used	BU	Proof
1990	2,761,431		£6.00	£7.00	£10.00
	Specimen in card/folder			£10.00	
	56,102	.925 sterling silver proof			£25.00
	2,750	.917 gold proof			no data

COMMEMORATIVE TYPE 2
Mary Gillick portrait of QEII
Design by: Robert Elderton
St. Edward's crown
Design by: Robert Elderton

			Used	BU	Proof
1993	1,834,655		£6.00	£7.00	£10.00
	Specimen in folder			£9.00	
	58,877*	.925 sterling silver proof			£25.00
	2,500	.917 gold proof			no data

* Oddly, a higher certificate with number 58,879 has been seen.

COMMEMORATIVE TYPE 3
Standard portrait of QE II
Design by: Raphael Maklouf
Windsor Castle and Pennants
Design by: Avril Vaughan
Edge:
VIVAT REGINA ELIZABETHA

		Used	BU	Proof
1996	2,396,100	£6.00	£7.00	£10.00
	Specimen in folder		£9.00	
75,000	.925 sterling silver proof			£25.00
2,750	.917 gold proof			£1,300.00

COMMEMORATIVE TYPE 4
Conjoined busts of Elizabeth II
and Prince Philip
Design by: Philip Nathan
Arms of the Royal Couple,
crown, anchor. Design by: Leslie
Durbin

		Used	BU	Proof
1997	1,733,000	£6.00	£7.00	£10.00
	Specimen in folder		£9.00	
33,689	.925 sterling silver proof			£25.00
2,750	.917 gold proof			£1,300.00

COMMEMORATIVE TYPE 5
Standard portrait of QE II
Design by: Ian Rank-Broadley
Prince Charles, "The Prince's Trust"
Design by: Michael Noakes

		Used	BU	Proof
1998	1,407,300	£6.00	£7.00	£10.00
43,465	Specimen in folder		£9.00	
35,000	.925 sterling silver proof			£25.00
2,000	.917 gold proof			£1,300.00

COMMEMORATIVE TYPE 6
Standard portrait of QEII
Design by: Ian Rank-Broadley
Portrait of Princess Diana
Design by: David Cornell

		Used	BU	Proof
1999	5,396,300 (for both 1999 crowns)	£6.00	£7.00	£9.00
358,991	Specimen in folder		£12.00	
49,545	.925 sterling silver proof			£35.00
2,750	.917 gold proof			£3,200.00

COMMEMORATIVE TYPE 7
Standard portrait of QE II
(Dated either 1999 or 2000)
Design by: Ian Rank-Broadley
Clock at midnight, with map
of the British Isles
Design by: Jeffrey Matthews
Edge:
WHAT'S PAST IS PROLOGUE

		Used	BU	Proof
Dated 1999 on Obverse	5,396,300 (inc. Type 6)	£6.00	£7.00	£10.00
	Specimen in folder		£12.00	
75,000	.925 sterling silver cased proof			£25.00
2,750	.917 gold cased proof			£1,300.00
Dated 2000 on Obverse (not shown)		£10.00	£15.00	£16.00
3,147,092*	Specimen in folder		£16.00	
75,000	.925 sterling silver proof			£40.00
2,750	.917 gold proof			£1,600.00

Exists with gold highlighted British Isles and clock hands, sold originally with a special £20 note.

COMMEMORATIVE TYPE 7a (SEE NEXT PAGE)

As above, with special dome mint-mark, available only at the Millennium Dome.
2000   Specimen in folder   £30.00

* Mintage is combined total for this coin and Type 8. Individual totals are not known.

TYPE 7a: Picture showing the location of the dome mint-mark, to the upper right of 'ANNO DOMINI'.

COMMEMORATIVE TYPE 8
Standard portrait of QE II
Design by: Ian Rank-Broadley
Portrait of the Queen Mother
Design by: Ian Rank-Broadley

		Used	BU	Proof
2000	3,147,092 (for both Type 8 and Type 7)	£6.00	£7.00	£10.00
	Specimen in folder		£10.00	
100,000	.925 sterling silver proof			£30.00
14,850	.925 sterling silver Piedfort proof			£35.00
2,750	.917 gold proof			£1,300.00

COMMEMORATIVE TYPE 9
Standard portrait of QEII
Design by: Ian Rank-Broadley
Wyon portrait of Victoria
Design by: Mary Milner Dickens

		Used	BU	Proof
2001	851,491	£6.00	£8.00	£10.00
	44,090 Specimen in folder		£11.00	
19,812	.925 sterling silver proof			£30.00
2,831	.917 gold proof			£1,400.00

COMMEMORATIVE TYPE 10
Queen Elizabeth II on horseback
Design by: Ian Rank-Broadley
Queen wearing robes and diadem
Design by: Ian Rank-Broadley

		Used	BU	Proof
2002	3,469,243	£6.00	£7.00	£10.00
	340,230	Specimen in folder	£10.00	
	54,012	.925 sterling silver proof		£30.00
	3,461	.917 gold proof		£1,400.00

COMMEMORATIVE TYPE 11
Standard portrait of QEII
Design by: Ian Rank-Broadley
Portrait of Queen Mother
Design by: Avril Vaughan.
Edge: STRENGTH DIGNITY LAUGHTER

		Used	BU	Proof
2002	Inc. above, with Type 10	£6.00	£7.00	£10.00
		Specimen in folder	£10.00	
	35,000	.925 sterling silver proof		£30.00
	2,750	.917 gold proof		£1,400.00

COMMEMORATIVE TYPE 12
Sketched portrait of QE II
Design by: Tom Philips
"GOD SAVE THE QUEEN"
Design by: Tom Philips

		Used	BU	Proof
2003	1,307,147	£6.00	£7.00	£10.00
	100,481	Specimen in folder	£10.00	
	75,000	.925 sterling silver proof		£30.00
	3,500	.917 gold proof		£1,400.00

38.61 mm • 28.28 grammes • cupro-nickel • milled edge

COMMEMORATIVE TYPE 13
Standard portrait of QEII
Design by: Ian Rank-Broadley
Conjoined Britannia and Marianne
Design by: David Gentlemen

			Used	BU	Proof
2004	1,205,594	(+ 16,507 in folders)	£6.00	£8.00	£10.00*
	11, 295 of 15k	.925 sterling silver proof			£30.00
	2,500	.925 sterling silver piedfort proof			£60.00
	926 of 1,500	.917 gold proof			£1,400.00
	501	.9995 platinum cased proof (3.0271 troy oz)			£3,800.00

* Was also sold as a cased base metal proof with certificate, value £20 - £25.

COMMEMORATIVE TYPE 14
Standard portrait of QE II
Design by: Ian Rank-Broadley
Portrait of Horatio Nelson
Design by: James Butler
Edge: ENGLAND EXPECTS EVERYMAN TO DO HIS DUTY

			Used	BU	Proof
2005	1,075,516 inc. Type 15		£6.00	£7.00	£10.00
	79,868	Specimen in folder		£11.00	
	12,852	.925 sterling silver proof			£30.00
	1,760	.917 gold proof			£1,400.00

COMMEMORATIVE TYPE 15
Standard portrait of QEII
Design by: Ian Rank-Broadley
HMS Victory & Temeraire
Design by: Clive Duncan

			Used	BU	Proof
2005	Inc. above, with Type 14		£6.00	£7.00	£10.00
	79,868	Specimen in folder		£11.00	
		Specimen set (contains both 2005 folders, in sleeve)		£25.00	
	21,448	.925 sterling silver proof			£30.00
	1,805	.917 gold proof			£1,400.00

COMMEMORATIVE TYPE 16
Standard portrait of QEII
Design by: Ian Rank-Broadley
Ceremonial Trumpets
with Banners
Design by:
Danuta Solowiej-Wedderburn
Edge: DUTY SERVICE FAITH

			Used	BU	Proof
2006	52,267		£7.00	£10.00	£10.00
	330,790	Specimen in folder		£12.00	
	20,790 of 50k	.925 sterling silver proof			£30.00
	5,000	.925 sterling silver piedfort proof			£60.00
	2,750	.917 gold proof			£1,500.00

COMMEMORATIVE TYPE 17
Standard portrait of QEII
Design by: Ian Rank-Broadley
The North Rose Window at
Westminster Abbey
Design by: Emma Noble
Edge: MY STRENGTH AND STAY

			Used	BU	Proof
2007	30,561		£7.00	£10.00	£10.00
	260,856	Specimen in folder		£12.00	
	15,186 of 35k	.925 sterling silver proof			£40.00
	2,000 of 5,000	.925 sterling silver piedfort proof			£60.00
	2,380 of 2,500	.917 gold proof			£1,500.00
	250	Platinum piedfort proof			£4,000.00

COMMEMORATIVE TYPE 18
Standard portrait of QEII
Design by: Ian Rank-Broadley
Portrait of Elizabeth I
Westminster Abbey
Design by: Rod Kelly
Edge: (proofs only)I HAVE
REIGNED WITH YOUR LOVES

		Used	BU	Proof
2008	20,047 'circulation' + 30,649 '£5 for £5'?	£7.00	£15.00	£18.00
26,700	Specimen in folder		£20.00	
9,216 of 20k	.925 sterling silver proof			£40.00
1,602 of 2k	.925 sterling silver piedfort proof			£60.00
1,500	.917 gold proof			£1,400.00
125 of 150	Platinum piedfort proof			£4,000.00

COMMEMORATIVE TYPE 19
Standard portrait of QEII
Design by: Ian Rank-Broadley
Portrait of the Price of Wales
Design by: Ian Rank-Broadley
Edge: SIXTIETH BIRTHDAY

		Used	BU	Proof
2008	14,088	£7.00	£15.00	£18.00
54,746	Specimen in folder		£17.00	
6,264	.925 sterling silver proof			£35.00
1088 of 5k	.925 sterling silver piedfort proof			£60.00
867 of 1500	.917 gold proof			£1,400.00
54 of 150	Platinum piedfort proof			£4,000.00

COMMEMORATIVE TYPE 20
Standard portrait of QEII
Design by: Ian Rank-Broadley
Henry VIII
Design by: John Bergdahl

		Used	BU	Proof
2009	(all originally sold in folders / proof sets)	£10.00	£15.00	£22.00
67,119	Specimen in folder		£20.00	
10,419 of 20k	.925 sterling silver proof			£35.00
3,580 of 4009	.925 sterling silver piedfort proof			£60.00
1130 of 1509	.917 gold proof			£1,500.00
100	Platinum piedfort proof			£4,000.00

COMMEMORATIVE TYPE 21
Standard portrait of QEII
Design by: Ian Rank-Broadley
Countdown '3'
Design by: Claire Aldridge

		Used	BU	Proof
2009	(all originally sold in folders / proof sets)	£8.00	£12.00	
184,921	Specimen in folder		£18.00	
26,645 of 30k	.925 sterling silver proof			£40.00
4,874 of 6k	.925 sterling silver piedfort proof			£60.00
1860 of 4000	.917 gold proof			£1,500.00

COMMEMORATIVE TYPE 22
Standard portrait of QEII
Design by: Ian Rank-Broadley
1660 Restoration of Monarchy
Design by: David Cornell
Obverse: Type as no. 20

		Used	BU	Proof
2010	(all originally sold in folders / proof sets)	£8.00	£12.00	£12.00
30,247	Specimen in folder		£18.00	
6,518 of 20k	.925 sterling silver proof			£30.00
4,435 of 5k	.925 sterling silver piedfort proof			£60.00
1,182 of 1,200	.917 gold proof			£1,500.00
100 max	Platinum piedfort proof			no data

COMMEMORATIVE TYPE 23
Standard portrait of QEII
Design by: Ian Rank-Broadley
Countdown '2'
Design by: Claire Aldridge

		Used	BU	Proof
2010	(all originally sold in folders)	£8.00	£12.00	
153,080	Specimen in folder		£15.00	
20,159 of 30k	.925 sterling silver proof			£50.00
4,435	.925 sterling silver piedfort proof			£60.00
1,562 of 3k	.917 gold proof			£1,500.00

As part of the Royal Mints unprecedented drive to make as many themed coins as possible, since becoming Royal Mint Ltd in 2010, higher face value coins were also issued. In silver: a £10 with a diameter of 65mm and weight of 5oz (155.5g) featuring the winged horse pegasus. A £500 with a diameter of 100mm and weight of one kilogram, featuring the stylised words 'XXX OLYMPIAD'.

Gold olympic themed coins consisted of 6x £25 coins (2 each for 'faster', 'higher' and 'stronger'), 3x £100 coins (one each for 'faster', 'higher' and 'stronger') and a crude looking one kilogram gold coin with a face value of £1000.

COMMEMORATIVE TYPE 24
Standard portrait of QEII
Design by: Ian Rank-Broadley
**Royal Wedding of William &
Catherine**
Design by: Mark Richards

		Used	BU	Proof
2011	(all originally sold in folders)	£8.00	£12.00	
250,000	Specimen in folder		£20.00	
26,069 of 50k	.925 sterling silver proof/ or 7,451 max gold plated coin*			£35.00
2,991 of 3k	.925 sterling silver piedfort proof			£80.00
2,066 of 3k	.917 gold proof			£1,500.00
133 of 200	Platinum piedfort proof			£4,000.00

*The previous gold plated maximum mintage of 3,000 seems to have been raised.

COMMEMORATIVE TYPE 25
Standard portrait of QEII
Design by: Ian Rank-Broadley
Countdown '1'
Design by: Claire Aldridge

		UNC	BU	Proof
2011	(all originally sold in folders)	£8.00	£12.00	
163,235	Specimen in folder		£15.00	
25,877 of 30k	.925 sterling silver proof			£35.00
4000	.925 sterling silver piedfort proof			£50.00
1,300 of 3k	.917 gold proof			£1,500.00

COMMEMORATIVE TYPE 26
Standard portrait of QEII
Design by: Ian Rank-Broadley
Prince Philip 90th Birthday
Design by: Mark Richards

		Used	BU	Proof
2011	(all originally sold in folders/proof sets)	£20.00	£35.00	£50.00
18,730	Specimen in folder		£40.00	
4,599 of 20k	.925 sterling silver proof			£60.00
2,659 of 4k	.925 sterling silver piedfort proof			£80.00
636 of 1,200	.917 gold proof			£1,600.00
49 of 90	Platinum piedfort proof			£4,000.00

COMMEMORATIVE TYPE 27
Standard portrait of QEII
Design by: Ian Rank-Broadley
Countdown '0'
Design by: Claire Aldridge

		Used	BU	Proof
2012	(all originally sold in folders)	£8.00	£12.00	
52,261*	Specimen in folder/card		£15.00	
12,670 of 30k	.925 sterling silver proof			£40.00
2,324 of 4k	.925 sterling silver piedfort proof			£80.00
1,007 of 3k	.917 gold proof			£1,600.00

* Plus 13,014 in packaging combining stamps with the coin.

COMMEMORATIVE TYPE 28
Standard portrait of QEII
Design by: Ian Rank-Broadley
London 2012 Olympics
Commemorative
Design by: Siaman Miah
Obverse: Type as no. 24

		Used	BU	Proof
2012	(all originally sold in folders)	£10.00	£14.00	
315,983*	Specimen in folder		£15.00	
20,810 of 100k	.925 sterling silver proof			£30.00
5,946 of 7k	.925 sterling silver piedfort proof			£100.00
8,180 of 12.5k	.925 sterling silver, gold plating*			£50.00
1,045 of 5k	.917 gold proof			£1,700.00

* Plus 13,959 in packaging combining stamps with the coin.

20x 2012 £1000 face value gold Olympic games coins were sold. Other proof gold coins included six classical Olympics themed £25 coins and three £100 coins. Full sets are still available new for £10,500. 5,056 5oz silver coins were sold and 910x £500FV 1kg coins were sold.

COMMEMORATIVE TYPE 29
Standard portrait of QEII
Design by: Ian Rank-Broadley
London 2012 Paralympics
Commemorative
Design by: Pippa Sanderson
Obverse: Type as no. 24

		Used	BU	Proof
2012	(all originally sold in folders)	£8.00	£25.00	
50,143*	Specimen in folder		£25.00	
10,000/3,000*	.925 sterling silver proof / or gold plated version			£40.00
2012 max	.925 sterling silver piedfort proof			£65.00
5000 max	.917 gold proof			no data

* Plus 13,014 in packaging combining stamps with the coin.

COMMEMORATIVE TYPE 30
Special portrait of QEII
Design by: Ian Rank-Broadley
Queen's Diamond Jubilee
Design by: Ian Rank-Broadley

		Used	BU	Proof
2012			£8.00	£12.00
	(961 base metal proofs sold separately)			£12.00
484,775*	Specimen in folder		£10.00	
16,820 of 75k	.925 sterling silver proof			£40.00
3,187 of 3,250	.925 sterling silver piedfort proof			£50.00
12,112 of 12.5k	.925 sterling silver, gold plated*			no data
1,085 of 3,850	.917 gold proof			£1,700.00
20 of 250	Platinum piedfort proof			no data

To mark the Jubilee there was also a £10 coin (as silver or gold proof) with a diameter of 65mm - these have the same obverse as above and feature the queen enthroned and facing on the reverse. Prices new were about £450 for the silver version (1933 sold) and £9,500 for the gold coin (they sold 140). One kilogram silver (£500FV, 206 sold) and one kilogram gold (£1000FV, 21 sold) coins were also made to mark the Queens jubilee. Both use the same obverse as above and show the full Royal Arms on the reverse.

* Plus 18,948 in packages combining stamps with the coin.

COMMEMORATIVE TYPE 31
Standard portrait of QEII
Design by: Ian Rank-Broadley
Anniversary of Coronation
Design by: Emma Noble
Obverse: Type as no. 24

		Used	BU	Proof
2013	(all originally sold in folders/proof sets)	£8.00	£12.00	£20.00
57,262*	Specimen in folder		£20.00	
6,667 of 15k	.925 sterling silver proof			£40.00
3,185 of 3,250	.925 sterling silver piedfort proof			£500.00
2,547 of 12.5k	.925 sterling silver, gold plated			£50.00
458 of 2,000	.917 gold proof, price new			no data
106 of 100 max!	Platinum piedfort proof, price new			no data

*Plus 11,642 in packages combining stamps with the coin.
301 x £500 1kg silver proofs were sold. 1604 x 5oz silver proofs were also sold.

32a

32b

COMMEMORATIVE TYPES 32a & 32b

Standard portrait of QEII
Design by: Ian Rank-Broadley
32a: Birth of Prince George
32b: Christening of Prince George
Design by: Benedetto Pistrucci (Birth). John Bergdahl (Christening)
Obverses: Both as Type no. 23

			Used	BU	Proof
2013	7,460*	(32a) .925 sterling silver proof only			£110.00
		(32b)	£10.00	£14.00	
	56,014	(32b) Specimen in folder	£17.00		
	7,264 of 75k	(32b) .925 sterling silver proof			£30.00
	2,251 of 2.5k	(32b) .925 sterling silver piedfort proof			£70.00
	486 of 1000	(32b) .917 gold proof			£1,700.00
	38 of 100	(32b) Platinum piedfort proof			no data

*Shortly after the birth of Prince George, a silver proof only £5 Crown was released with the Pistrucci St. George Reverse. This was the first coin that the Royal Mint refused to sell to other businesses, offering it exclusively to their customers for £80. Apparently 25 platinum proof versions of the birth coin were also made.

Note that for both the 2013 coronation (no. 31) and Prince George (no.32b) one kilo versions with a face value of £500 were struck in silver. These were both available new for £2600. Gold kilo versions of no. 32b were also sold.

COMMEMORATIVE TYPE 33

Standard portrait of QEII
Design by: Ian Rank-Broadley
300th Anniversary of the Death of Queen Anne
Design by: Mark Richards
Obverse: Type as no. 24

			Used	BU	Proof
2014		(all originally sold in folders/proof sets)	£25.00	£35.00	£35.00
	12,181	Specimen in folder		£60.00	
	2,212 of 3,100	.925 sterling silver proof			£70.00
	627 of 1,665	.925 sterling silver, gold plated			£80.00
[was 2014 max]	4,028 max*	.925 sterling silver piedfort proof			£100.00
	253 of 375	.917 gold proof, price new			£1,800.00
	250 max?	Platinum piedfort proof			no data

* 636 were sold.

129

COMMEMORATIVE TYPE 34
Standard portrait of QEII
Design by: Ian Rank-Broadley
Re-used 1953/1960 reverse to
mark the 1st birthday
of Prince George
Design by:
Edgar Fuller & Cecil Thomas
Edge: Milled

Proof

2014		
7,451 of 7,500	.925 sterling silver proof only	£70-£90

COMMEMORATIVE TYPE 35
Standard portrait of QEII
Design by: Ian Rank-Broadley
Winston Churchill - 50th Anniversary of his death
Design by: Mark Richards
Obverse: Type as no. 24
Edge (on proofs): NEVER FLINCH, NEVER WEARY,
NEVER DESPAIR

		Used	BU	Proof
2015		£8.00	£12.00	£15.00
18,163*	Specimen in folder		£15.00	
7,500 max	.925 sterling silver proof			£40.00
2,000 max	.925 sterling silver piedfort proof			£60.00
275 of 620	.917 gold proof, price new			£1,800.00
65 max	Platinum piedfort proof			no data

* Plus a further 4,987 sold in packs including the 1965 Churchill Crown (sourced 2nd hand) and 9,896 in packs including new commemorative Royal Mail stamps.

COMMEMORATIVE TYPE 36a and 36b
Standard portrait of QEII
Design by: Ian Rank-Broadley (36a) or Jody Clark (36b)
Battle of Waterloo - 200th Anniversary
Design by: David Lawrence
Obverse: Type as no. 24 (for 36a) or as no. 41 (for 36b)
Edge (on proofs): THE NEAREST RUN THING YOU EVER SAW

			Used	BU	Proof
2015	24,554*	(36a) Loose coin, ex pack	£8.00	£12.00	£12.00
		(36a) Specimen in folder		£20.00	
	3,000 max	(36b) .925 sterling silver proof			£50.00
	1500 max	(36a) .925 sterling silver proof, part of set of 5 coins			£100.00?
	1500 max	(36b) .925 sterling silver piedfort proof			£75.00
	500 max	(36b) .917 gold proof, price new			£1,945.00

The individually boxed silver proof coins of this type (36b) feature the 5th portrait. Some were also made as silver proof with the 4th portrait, available only in sets of 5x 2015 silver proof coins. A £2 coin with a diameter of 38.61mm, featuring the reverse design of the Waterloo coin was also sold as part of a set of three Waterloo commemorative coins marketed by the Dutch Mint.

* Plus another 8,576 sold in packs including new commemorative Royal Mail stamps.

COMMEMORATIVE TYPE 37
Standard portrait of QEII
Design by: Jody Clark
Birth of Princess Charlotte
Design by: John Bergdahl
Edge: Milled (non proof)

			Used	BU	Proof
2015			£8.00	£30.00	£30.00
	30,926	Specimen in folder		£35.00	
	4,500 max	.925 sterling silver proof			£50.00
	250 max	.917 gold proof, price new			£1,800.00

See also COMMEMORATIVE TYPE 39 for the Princess Charlotte Christening coin.

38.61 mm • 28.28 grammes • cupro-nickel • various edge

COMMEMORATIVE TYPE 38
Alternative portrait of QEII
Design by: James Butler
Longest Reigning Monarch
Design by: James Butler
Edge (on precious metal proofs):
LONG TO REIGN OVER US

		Used	BU	Proof
2015	48,848 (all originally sold in folders)	£8.00	£12.00	
	Specimen in folder		£15.00	
9,000 max	.925 sterling silver proof			£40.00
3,700 max	.925 sterling silver piedfort proof			£60.00
1650 max	.917 gold proof, price new			£1,400.00
63 max	.Platinum proof, price new			no data

See also the Longest Reigning Monarch £20 coin, the design of which was also used on larger size silver and gold proof coins, which were very expensive new and are rarely offered.

COMMEMORATIVE TYPE 39
Standard Fifth portrait of QEII
Design by: Jody Clark
Christening of
Princess Charlotte
Design by: John Bergdahl
Edge: Milled

		Proof
2015		
4,500 max	.925 sterling silver proof only	£60.00

COMMEMORATIVE TYPE 40
Standard Fifth portrait of QEII
Design by: Jody Clark
Second Birthday of
Prince George
Design by: Christopher Le Brun
Obverse: Same as TYPE 39
Edge: Milled

		Proof
2015		
7,500 max	.925 sterling silver proof only	£100.00

COMMEMORATIVE TYPE 41
Standard Fifth portrait of QEII
Design by: Jody Clark
Queen's 90th Birthday
Design by: Christopher Hobbs
Edge (on precious metal proofs):
FULL OF HONOUR AND YEARS

		Used	BU	Proof
2016	74,195 (only sold in folders / sets)	£8.00	£8.00	£10.00
8,947 of 13k	.925 sterling silver proof			£35.00
3,099 of 7k	.925 sterling silver piedfort proof			£50.00
906 of 1200	.917 gold proof			£1,400.00
77 of 90	Platinum piedfort proof			no data

This coin design was also used for 5oz silver, gold and 1kg silver coins. They are rarely offered. A further 10,181 BU coins were sold in tubes to other retailers.

COMMEMORATIVE TYPE 42
Standard Fifth portrait of QEII
Design by: Jody Clark
King Canute
Design by: Lee R. Jones
Edge (on precious metal proofs):
TIME AND TIDE WAIT FOR NO MAN

		Used	BU	Proof
2017	26,567 (only sold in folders / proof sets)	£8.00	£12.00	£16.00
2,952? of 3k	.925 sterling silver proof, price new			£82.50
1,071? of 1,500	.925 sterling silver piedfort proof, price new			£155.00
150?	.917 gold proof, price new			£1945.00

COMMEMORATIVE TYPE 43
Standard Fifth portrait of QEII
Design by: Jody Clark
House of Windsor
Design by: Timothy Noad
Edge (on precious metal proofs):
THE CHRISTENING OF A DYNASTY

		Used	BU	Proof
2017	29,116 (only sold in folders / proof sets)	8.00	£12.00	£16.00
10,000 max.	.925 sterling silver proof, price new			£82.50
4,000 max.	.925 sterling silver piedfort proof, price new			£155.00
750 max.	.917 gold proof, price new			£1975.00

38.61 mm • 28.28 grammes • cupro-nickel • various edge

COMMEMORATIVE TYPE 44
Standard Fifth portrait of QEII
Design by: Jody Clark
Sapphire Jubilee
Design by:
Edge (on precious metal proofs):
SHINE THROUGH THE AGES

		Used	BU	Proof
2017	74k+ (only sold in folders / proof sets)	£8.00	£13.00	£16.00
	8,600 max. .925 sterling silver proof			£30.00
	2,500 max. .925 sterling silver piedfort proof			£50.00
	650 max. .917 gold proof			£1,400.00

Other 'Sapphire Jubilee' coins were also made available.

COMMEMORATIVE TYPE 45
Standard Fifth portrait of QEII
Design by: Etienne Millner
Royal Wedding Anniversary
Design by: John Bergdahl
Edge (on precious metal proofs):
FELICES JUNXIT CONUBIALIS
AMOR

		Used	BU	Proof
2017	40k+ (only sold in folders / proof sets)	£9.00	£13.00	£16.00
	15,000 max .925 sterling silver proof			£35.00
	4,000 .925 sterling silver piedfort proof			£70.00
	1,250 max. .917 gold proof			£1,400.00

5oz silver and 5oz gold proof coins as well as 1kg silver and 1kg gold proof coins were also made for the Royal Wedding anniversary, both featuring different designs.

 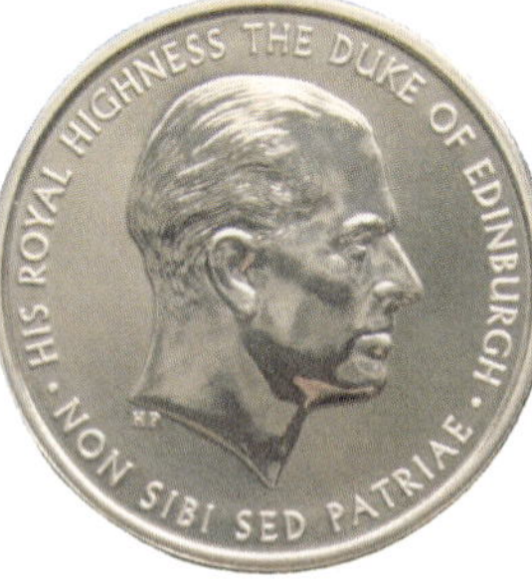

COMMEMORATIVE TYPE 46
Standard Fifth portrait of QEII
Design by: Jody Clark
Service of Prince Philip
Design by: T 'Humphrey' Paget
Edge: Milled for base metal -
Plain on precious metal proofs.

		Used	BU	Proof
2017	29,097 (only sold in folders / proof sets)	£10.00	£15.00	£16.00
	3,000 max. .925 sterling silver proof			£40.00
	1,250 max. .925 sterling silver piedfort proof			£80.00
	350 max. .917 gold proof			£1,500.00

COMMEMORATIVE TYPE 47
Standard Fifth portrait of QEII
Design by: Jody Clark
Remembrance Day 2017
Design by: Stephen Taylor
Edge: Milled (all types)

		BU	Proof
2017	(all originally sold in folders)	£30.00	
5,000 max.	.925 sterling silver proof, price new		£50.00
1,500 max.	.925 sterling silver piedfort proof, price new		£155.00

COMMEMORATIVE TYPE 48
Standard Fifth portrait of QEII
Design by: Jody Clark
Christmas 2017
Design by: Edwina Ellis
Edge: Milled

		BU
2017	38k+ (only sold within a blank Christmas card), price new	£13.00

COMMEMORATIVE TYPE 49
Standard Fifth portrait of QEII
Design by: Jody Clark
Prince George's fifth birthday
Design by: Jody Clark
Edge: Milled on all versions

		Used	BU	Proof
2018	(all originally sold in folders/proof sets)	£9.00	£12.00	£16.00

135

COMMEMORATIVE TYPE 50
Standard Fifth portrait of QEII
Design by: Jody Clark
4 Generations of Royal Family
Design by: Timothy Noad
Edge: Milled for base metal
(Precious metal edges are plain)

		Used	BU	Proof
2018	(all originally sold in folders / proof sets)	£9.00	£13.00	£16.00
5,000 max.	.925 sterling silver proof			£55.00
2,000 max.	.925 sterling silver piedfort proof, price new			£155.00
500 max.	.917 gold proof, price new			£1,975.00
1,000 max.	.925 sterling silver 5oz £10 coin (larger), price new			£415.00
1,100 max.	.917 gold proof 1/4oz £25 coin (smaller), price new			£475.00
100 max.	.917 gold proof 5oz £10 coin (larger), price new			£8,450.00

Just in case the base metal version plus the usual silver and gold proofs of this rather uninspired design (no disrespect to the designer) simply wasn't enough for you, fortunately there are another three different versions to satisfy your collecting needs!

I do wonder if they've got something wrong in the blurb on their website - the 1/4oz gold proof has a face value of £25 and the 5oz gold proof has a face value of £10? Surely if 0.25oz is £25 then 5oz should be £500? Perhaps they used an incorrect obverse picture showing the wrong face value.

COMMEMORATIVE TYPE 51
Standard Fifth portrait of QEII
Design by: Jody Clark
65th Anniversary of Coronation
Design by: Stephen Taylor
Edge (on precious metal proofs):
SHINE THROUGH THE AGES

		Used	BU	Proof
2018	(all originally sold in folders)	£9.00	£13.00	
6,500 max	.925 sterling silver proof, price new			£82.50
1,953 max	.925 sterling silver piedfort proof			£160.00
550 max	.917 gold proof, price new			£1,980.00

Further coins were also made to mark 65 years since the coronation. They include a £10 gold proof, £10 silver proof, £500 silver kilo and £25 1/4oz gold coin.

COMMEMORATIVE TYPE 52
Standard Fifth portrait of QEII
Design by: Jody Clark
Wedding of Harry & Meghan
Design by: Jody Clark
Edge: Milled for base metal
(Precious metal edges are plain)

	Used	BU	Proof
2018 (all originally sold in folders)	£9.00	£13.00	
15,000 max — .925 sterling silver proof			£100.00
2,018 max — .925 sterling silver piedfort proof, price new			£155.00
.917 gold proof, price new			£1,980.00

COMMEMORATIVE TYPE 53
Standard Fifth portrait of QEII
Design by: Jody Clark
Remembrance Poppy 2018
Design by: Laura Clancy
Edge: Milled on all versions

	Used	BU	Proof
2018 (all originally sold in folders)	£10.00	£17.00	
3,500 max — .925 sterling silver proof, price new			£90.00
1,500 max — .925 sterling silver piedfort proof, price new			£170.00

COMMEMORATIVE TYPE 54
Standard Fifth portrait of QEII
Design by: Jody Clark
Prince Charles 70th Birthday
Design by: Robert Elderton
Edge: Milled for base metal
(Precious metal edges are plain)

	Used	BU	Proof
2018 (all originally sold in folders)	£9.00	£13.00	
4,500 max — .925 sterling silver proof			£60.00
1,000 max — .925 sterling silver piedfort proof, price new			£155.00
300 max — .917 gold proof, price new			£1,995.00
70 max — .9995 platinum piedfort proof, price new			£4,000.00

Also available in a smaller, platinum 1/4oz £25 guise.

COMMEMORATIVE TYPE 55
Standard Fifth portrait of QEII
Design by: Jody Clark
Christmas 2018 coin
Design by: Harry Brockway
Edge: Milled

BU

2018	(all originally sold within a blank Christmas card)	£13.00

COMMEMORATIVE TYPE 56
Standard Fifth portrait of QEII
Design by: Jody Clark
200th Anniversary of the
birth of Queen Victoria
Design by: John Bergdahl
Edge (on precious metal proofs):
WORKSHOP OF THE WORLD

		BU	Proof
2019	(all originally sold in folders/proof sets)	£13.00	£16.00
	.925 sterling silver proof, price new		£82.50
	.925 sterling silver piedfort proof, price new		£155.00
	.917 gold proof, price new		£1,975.00

COMMEMORATIVE TYPE 57
Standard Fifth portrait of QEII
Design by: Jody Clark
Remembrance Poppy 2019
Design by: Harry Brockway
Edge: Milled on all versions

		BU	Proof
2019	(all originally sold in folders)	£17.00	
	.925 sterling silver proof, price new		£90.00
	.925 sterling silver piedfort proof, price new		£155.00
	.917 gold proof, price new		£2,295.00

The 2019 coin that never came
A 2019 Christmas themed coin was planned, but never materialised.

COMMEMORATIVE TYPE 58
Standard Fifth portrait of QEII
Design by: Jody Clark
(as type 56, dated 2020)
200th Anniversary since end
of George III's reign
Design by: Dominique Evans
Edge: (on precious metal proofs)
I GLORY IN THE NAME OF
BRITON

		BU	Proof
2020	(all originally sold in folders/proof sets)	£13.00	£16.00
2,500 max	.925 sterling silver proof, price new		£82.50
550 max	.925 sterling silver piedfort proof, price new		£155.00
250 max	.917 gold proof, price new		£2,295.00

£5 coins that don't commemorate royal events or were only made available in precious metals, are now found here, in part 2 of the Five Pounds section

CELEBRATION OF BRITAIN: Mind, Body and Spirit (2009 and 2010)

The Royal Mint issued a whopping eighteen different crowns in conjunction with the London 2012 Olympics, eleven of which are shown on the following pages. Starting in June 2009, one was issued every twenty-eight days until late 2010. The eighteen coins were made available as a complete set (one of which, with original packaging, box etc sold for nearly £900.00) as well as being available in groups of six (themed: 'Mind', 'Body' and 'Spirit').

They were all struck as sterling silver proofs. Three of them: the Clock-face (1), London (15) and Churchill (16) coins were also struck in cupro-nickel. The obverse design is the same as that used for COMMEMORATIVE TYPE 24, but dated either 2009 or 2010, as indicated. The reverse designs are all of a high standard and by Shane Greeves. Each design is accompanied by some wise words with a very loose connection to the subject matter of the designs featured.

CAUTION: Chinese made forgeries of this series exist. The fakes have inconsistently frosted details and poorly executed colouring of the '2012' logos.

CELEBRATION TYPE 1
Mind Series (with green London 2012 logo)
Clock-face of the Palace of Westminster
Walter Bagehot quote:
"Nations touch at their summits"

2009	.925 Sterling silver proof (95k max.)	£30-£40
2009	Cupro-Nickel proof (100k max.)	£20-£25

CELEBRATION TYPE 2
Mind Series (with green London 2012 logo)
Stonehenge
William Blake quote:
"Great things are done when men and mountains meet"

2009	.925 Sterling silver proof (95k max.)	£30-£40

CELEBRATION TYPE 2
Mind Series (with green London 2012 logo)
The Angel of the North
William Shakespeare quote:
"I have touched the highest point of all my greatness"

2009	.925 Sterling silver proof (95k max.)	£30-£40

CELEBRATION TYPE 4
Mind Series (with green London 2012 logo)
The Flying Scotsman
William Shakespeare quote:
"True hope is swift"

2009 .925 Sterling silver proof (95k max.) £30-£40

CELEBRATION TYPE 5
Mind Series (with green London 2012 logo)
Sculpture of Isaac Newton
William Shakespeare quote:
"Make not your thoughts your prisons"

2009 .925 Sterling silver proof (95k max.) £30-£40

CELEBRATION TYPE 6
Mind Series (with green London 2012 logo)
The Globe Theatre
William Shakespeare quote:
"We are such stuff as dreams are made of"

2009 .925 Sterling silver proof (95k max.) £30-£40

CELEBRATION TYPE 7
Body Series (with red London 2012 logo)
Rhossili Bay
William Blake quote:
"To see a world in a grain of sand"

2010 .925 Sterling silver proof (95k max.) £30-£40

CELEBRATION TYPE 8
Body Series (with red London 2012 logo)
Giant's Causeway
Alice Oswald quote:
"When the stone began to dream"

2010 .925 Sterling silver proof (95k max.) £30-£40

38.61 mm • 28.28 grammes • cupro-nickel • various edge

Celebration of Britain: Mind, Body and Spirit 2009 - 2010 (continued).

CELEBRATION TYPE 9
Body Series (with red London 2012 logo)
The River Thames
Percy Bysshe Shelley quote:
"Tameless, and swift, and proud"

2010   .925 Sterling silver proof (95k max.)   £30-£40

CELEBRATION TYPE 10
Body Series (with red London 2012 logo)
Barn Owl
Samuel Johnson quote:
"The natural flights of the human mind"

2010   .925 Sterling silver proof (95k max.)   £30-£40

CELEBRATION TYPE 11
Body Series (with red London 2012 logo)
Oak leaves and an acorn
Alfred, Lord Tennyson quote:
"To strive, to seek ... and not to yield"

2010   .925 Sterling silver proof (95k max.)   £30-£40

CELEBRATION TYPE 12
Body Series (with red London 2012 logo)
Weather-vane
Charlotte Brontë quote:
"Never may a cloud come o'er the sunshine of your mind"

2010   .925 Sterling silver proof (95k max.)   £30-£40

CELEBRATION TYPE 13
Spirit Series (with blue London 2012 logo)
Floral emblems of the UK
John Lennon quote:
"And the world will be as one"

2010   .925 Sterling silver proof (95k max.)   £30-£40

CELEBRATION TYPE 14
Spirit Series (with blue London 2012 logo)
White rabbit from Alice in Wonderland
T S Elliot quote:
"All touched by a common genius"

2010   .925 Sterling silver proof (95k max.)   £30-£40

CELEBRATION TYPE 15
Spirit Series (with blue London 2012 logo)
View down the Mall, London
Alfred, Lord Tennyson quote:
"Kind hearts are more than coronets"

2010   .925 Sterling silver proof (95k max.)   £30-£40
2010   Cupro-Nickel proof (100k max.)   £20-£25

CELEBRATION TYPE 16
Spirit Series (with blue London 2012 logo)
Winston Churchill Statue
Anita Roddick quote:
"Be daring, be first, be different, be just"

2010   .925 Sterling silver proof (95k max.)   £30-£40
2010   Cupro-Nickel proof (100k max.)   £20-£25

CELEBRATION TYPE 17
Spirit Series (with blue London 2012 logo)
Musical instruments sculpture
Lennon & McCartney quote:
"All you need is love"

2010   .925 Sterling silver proof (95k max.)   £30-£40

CELEBRATION TYPE 18
Spirit Series (with blue London 2012 logo)
Image of campaigner Equiano
William Shakespeare quote:
"To thine own self be true"

2010   .925 Sterling silver proof (95k max.)   £30-£40

THE QUEEN'S PORTRAIT SET (2013)

Reverse

Gillick Obverse

Machin Obverse

Coins featuring the four Portraits of the Queen used on coinage -
Three previous obverses and the current obverse of the time,
by: Mary Gillick, Arnold Machin, Raphael Maklouf and Ian Rank-Broadley
Reverse Design (common to all), the Royal Arms by: James Butler

This set of four coins produced in 2013, available only in sets struck in either .925 silver or .917 gold. All four coins share the same reverse. The obverses used are as follows:
Coin 1: A re-worked Mary Gillick obverse with 'FIVE POUNDS' under the bust.
Coin 2: A re-worked Arnold Machin obverse with new legend to incorporate 'FIVE POUNDS'.
Coin 3: Appears to be the same reverse as used on the 1990 Crown (Commemorative Type 1).
Coin 4: One of the standard obverses of the time which first appeared on the 2002 Crown (Commemorative Type 11).

Proof

| 2013 | 1,465 of 4,800 max | .925 silver proof set of 4, price new | £400.00 |
| | 150 of 450 | .917 gold proof set of 4, price new | £7,200.00 |

THE PORTRAIT OF BRITAIN SET (2014)

In 2014 a set of four .925 sterling silver proof coins dubbed 'The Portrait of Britain Collection' was sold new for £360.00. The reverses by Glyn Davies and Laura Clancy featured Tri-Chromatic pad printed images of The Elizabeth Tower (Big Ben), Buckingham Palace, Tower Bridge and Trafalgar Square. Maximum mintage was 3,500 (1,299 were sold). Sorry, no pictures yet!

THE FIRST WORLD WAR, SIX COIN SET (2014)

And if that wasn't enough, the first set of six .925 sterling silver proof only coins were produced to mark WWI, using the same obverse type as COMMEMORATIVE TYPE 24 . This set was £450.00 new and a maximum of 1914 complete sets were produced (839 were sold). Sorry, no pictures yet!

FIRST WORLD WAR, SIX COIN SET (2015)

Albert Ball VC   Animals at war   Submarines

Edith Cavell   Merchant Navy   Gallipoli

The second set of six coins produced to mark WWI, struck in .925 silver. All six coins share the same obverse (the same used on Commemorative Type 41. The reverses used are as follows:

Coin 1: Albert Ball VC, by David Cornell. Edge: BY FAR THE BEST ENGLISH FLYING MAN.
Coin 2: Animals at war, by David Lawrence. Edge: PATIENT EYES COURAGEOUS HEARTS.
Coin 3: Submarines, by Edwina Ellis. Edge: IN LITTLE BOXES MADE OF TIN.
Coin 4: Edith Cavell, by David Cornell. Edge: SHE FACED THEM GENTLE AND BOLD.
Coin 5: Merchant Navy, by David Rowlands. Edge: SEPULCHRED IN THE HARBOUR OF THE DEEP.
Coin 6: Gallipoli, by John Bergdahl. Edge: HEROES THAT SHED THEIR BLOOD.

			Proof
2015	1,915 max	.925 silver proof set of 6, price new	£465.00

Maximum mintage for each coin was marked as 2,500 with the exception of the Gallipoli coin, which was 5,000. This would imply that the coins also appear singly and not just in sets of six. They don't seem to have been very popular though, as they are still available at the end of 2016 and the Royal Mint offered them at a discount through their eBay account - I was able to purchase a set for about £260.00, hence the more extensive coverage and my own photographs on this page!

145

THE PORTRAIT OF BRITAIN SET (2016)

In 2016 a second (the first set was sold in 2014) set of four .925 sterling silver proof coins dubbed 'Portrait of Britain 2016 UK £5 Silver Collection' was sold new for £295.00. The reverses by Glyn Davies and Laura Clancy feature Tri-Chromatic pad printed images of The White Cliffs of Dover, Giants Causeway, Lake District and Snowdonia. 1,098 out of a maximum mintage of 2,016 were sold. Interesting to note the reductions in both price and mintage over the 2014 set. Sorry, no pictures yet!

FIRST WORLD WAR, SIX COIN SET (2016)

And another set of six coins produced in 2016, the third set to mark WWI, struck in .925 silver. All six coins share the same obverse (the same used on Commemorative Type 41.) Themes of the six coins are 'The Boy Hero of Jutland (Jack Cornwell)', 'The Battle of Jutland', 'Dreadnought', 'The Somme', 'The Army', and 'Poetry and Language'. The Somme coin was available separately and is shown on the next page as Commemorative Type 'Somme'.

			Proof
2016	499 of 1,916	.925 silver proof set of 6, price new	£450.00
2016	25 of 450	.917 gold proof set of 6, price new	£10,500.00

The Royal Mint have produced rather a lot of silver-proof-only £5 coins over the last few years. They are a business (at least, the commemorative coins side of things is a business) and their imperative is to make as much profit as possible. Clearly they make more profit selling silver proof £5 crown coins for around £75 - £80 each, than they do producing larger numbers of base metal £5 crown coins and selling them for around £13 in card packaging.

Gone are the days where you used to be able to buy a bog-standard £5 crown coin for £5*. To me, if a coin never circulates, isn't actually meant to circulate and doesn't even exist in a standard circulation form (not even in base metal) and the only way you can get one is by buying it new, then it's not a coin at all in the strictest sense, it's simply a medal with a denomination marked on it. The Royal Mint have a huge advantage in that they can create as many products as they like and basically have the exclusive right to mark any denomination on them as they care to.

The public no longer have the pleasure of discovering new crowns in change or at their local Post Office/bank and if people did want to own them all, they'd have to shell out a large sum of money each year. I feel that is financially out of reach for most.

* Not to be confused with the other offers from different companies of £5 coins for £5, which are nearly always coins marked as £5 made for tiny islands and territories, rather than proper legal tender UK coinage and/or are simply ploys to get you on a mailing list.

COMMEMORATIVE TYPE SOMME
Standard Fifth portrait of QEII
Design by: Jody Clark
Battle of the Somme, 100th Anniversary.
Design by: John Bergdahl
Edge:
DEAD MEN CAN ADVANCE NO FURTHER
Obverse: As Type 41.

Proof

2016

	3,678 of 6k	.925 sterling silver proof only, price new	£82.50

*Apparently the boxed proof coins are limited to 1,916. The total maximum mintage is 6,000. I'm not sure how the others were sold.

THE PORTRAIT OF BRITAIN SET (2017)

In 2017 a third set of four .925 sterling silver proof coins (max. mintage 1,500) dubbed 'Portrait of Britain 2017 UK £5 Silver Collection' was sold new originally for £295.00 (they are still available mid-2020, now for £350). The reverses by Glyn Davies and Laura Clancy feature Tri-Chromatic pad printed images of Downing Street, Edinburgh Castle, Hampton Court Palace and Westminster Abbey. Maximum mintage is apparently 1,500. Sorry, no pictures yet!

FIRST WORLD WAR, SIX COIN SET (2017)

And the fourth set of six coins produced in 2017 to mark WWI, struck in .925 silver. All six coins share the same obverse (the same used on Commemorative Type 41.) Themes of the six coins are 'Noel Chavasse', 'Medical Services', 'Sopwith Camel', 'Art and Poetry', 'Gas', and 'Battle of Arras'.

2017	1,917 max	.925 silver proof set of 6, price new	£465.00
2017	450 max	.917 gold proof set of 6, price new	£11,000.00

THE PORTRAIT OF BRITAIN SET (2018)

The 2018 Portrait of Britain set of four .925 silver proof coins (max. mintage 1,500) show: Tenby harbour with the inscription 'TENBY' Blackpool Tower with the inscription 'BLACKPOOL', a view of Brighton Pier with the inscription 'BRIGHTON' and a view of Southwold beach with the inscription "SOUTHWOLD".

This set is still available in mid-2020 for £350. Clearly not a big sales success and it looks like they've given up on them now, as there doesn't appear to have been 2019 or 2020 'Portrait of Britain' sets.

147

THE QUEEN'S BEASTS (2017 onwards)

Originally a silver bullion issue, these unexpectedly appeared in base-metal guise. There have been eight so far, out of an expected total of ten:

1. Lion of England (2017)
2. Unicorn of Scotland (2017)
3. Red Dragon of Wales (2018)
4. Black Bull of Clarence (2018)
5. Falcon of the Plantagenets (2019)
6. Yale of Beaufort (2019)
7. White Lion of Mortimer (2020)
8. White Horse of Hanover (2020)

All of the reverses are shown on the opposite page. The image below right shows the obverse, which is common to all.

The beasts depicted on the coins by Jody Clark, originally stood guard in statue form at the Queen's coronation in 1953. They are connected to a Royal event (the coronation) but don't actually commemorate it, so I've decided to put them here, in part 2 of the £5 coin section.

Note that there are design differences for the silver / gold versions, including different marked face values, different arrangement of the legend and textured backgrounds. Each coin is available in many guises and to me, it does all seem to be rather complicated!

Base metal:
£5 coin, sold new in card packs for £13.00

Bullion Issues, new prices (struck to BU standard):
2 oz silver (£5 marked face value), available for about £45.00
10 oz silver (£10 marked face value), available for about
£160.00 - £200.00

Proof Issues, new prices (2020):
1 oz silver proof, sold new for £85.00
5 oz silver proof, sold new for £420.00
1/4 oz gold proof, sold new for £530.00
10 oz silver proof, sold new for £795.00
1 oz gold proof, sold new for £2,100.00
1kg silver proof, sold new for £2,050.00
5 oz gold proof, sold new for £9,995.00
1kg gold proof, sold new for A LOT

THE QUEEN'S BEASTS, Coins 1 to 8.

COMMEMORATIVE TYPE ACADEMY
Standard Fifth portrait of QEII
Design by: Jody Clark
250th Anniversary of the Royal Academy
of Arts
Design by: Sir David Chipperfield RA
Edge: Milled
Obverse: Same as that shown on previous page.

			BU	Proof
2018				
	12,000 max	Base metal version, not available directly*	£35.00	
	2,750 max	.925 sterling silver proof only, price new		£82.50

*In an unusual marketing tactic (which I personally hope is not repeated) this coin in BU form was not available to buy directly from the Royal Mint and instead, had to be purchased via a single third party. It was only about £11.00 to buy new but has increased in value since, caused no doubt by the usual factors that seem to play a role when certain coins sell out. Whether the value will stay this high, remains to be seen.

COMMEMORATIVE TYPE LION 2018
An unplanned, fairly spontaneous (from what I can tell) 2018 dated 'Lion of England' coin was sold in special packs to cash in on England doing better than was expected in the Football World Cup. The design used was the same as that for the 'Lion of England' Queen's Beast coin, as shown on the previous page. They were sold new for £13.00. The current value is around £15.00.

COMMEMORATIVE TYPE TOWER 2019 1 (of 4)
Standard Fifth portrait of QEII
Design by: Jody Clark
Tower of London Raven
Design by: Glyn Davies
Edge: (on proofs) ON INTO TWILIGHT WITHIN WALLS OF STONE.

			BU	Proof
2019	(all originally sold in folders)		£13.00	
	4,000 max	.925 sterling silver proof, price new		£82.50
	950 max	.925 sterling silver piedfort proof, price new		£155.00
	325 max	.917 gold proof, price new		£2,495.00
	800 max (£25 face value)	.917 gold 1/4oz proof (smaller), price new		£480.00

This raven coin is one of four that will be sold to commemorate the Tower of London (in 2019 - another four came in 2020!). The other 2019 coins, shown on the next page, are themed 'The Crown Jewels' (available from March 2019), 'The Yeoman Warders' (June 2019) and 'The Ceremony of the Keys' (August 2019). 5oz silver proof and 5oz gold proof versions (both with £10 face value) were also sold.

COMMEMORATIVE TYPE
TOWER 2019 2 (of 4)
Standard Fifth portrait of QEII
Design by: Jody Clark
Crown and wall diagram
Design by: Glyn Davies
Edge: (on proofs) ON INTO TWILIGHT WITHIN WALLS OF STONE.

		BU	Proof
2019	(all originally sold in folders)	£13.00	
3,800 max	.925 sterling silver proof, price new		£82.50
950 max	.925 sterling silver piedfort proof, price new		£155.00
325 max	.917 gold proof, price new		£2,495.00
800 max (£25 face value)	.917 gold 1/4oz proof (smaller), price new		£555.00

COMMEMORATIVE TYPE
TOWER 2019 3 (of 4)
Standard Fifth portrait of QEII
Design by: Jody Clark
Crown and wall diagram
Design by: Glyn Davies
Edge: (on proofs) ON INTO TWILIGHT WITHIN WALLS OF STONE.

		BU	Proof
2019	(all originally sold in folders)	£13.00	
3,800 max	.925 sterling silver proof, price new		£82.50
950 max	.925 sterling silver piedfort proof, price new		£155.00
325 max	.917 gold proof, price new		£2,495.00
800 max (£25 face value)	.917 gold 1/4oz proof (smaller), price new		£555.00

COMMEMORATIVE TYPE
TOWER 2019 4 (of 4)
Standard Fifth portrait of QEII
Design by: Jody Clark
Crown and wall diagram
Design by: Glyn Davies
Edge: (on proofs) ON INTO TWILIGHT WITHIN WALLS OF STONE.

		BU	Proof
2019	(all originally sold in folders)	£13.00	
3,800 max	.925 sterling silver proof, price new		£82.50
950 max	.925 sterling silver piedfort proof, price new		£155.00
325 max	.917 gold proof, price new		£2,495.00
800 max (£25 face value)	.917 gold 1/4oz proof (smaller), price new		£555.00

COMMEMORATIVE TYPE LION 2019

Another spontaneous re-issue of the 'Lion of England' design (top left on page 149), this time to cash-in in on England winning the Cricket World Cup. Current value seems to be around £25.00.

COMMEMORATIVE TYPE YEAR OF THE RAT

Standard Fifth portrait of QEII
Design by: Jody Clark
Rat and Chinese symbol
Design by: P J Lynch
Edge: Milled on all versions.

		BU	Proof
2020	(all originally sold in folders)	£13.00	
2,588 max	.925 sterling silver 1oz proof, price new		£85.00

The original Lunar series of coins were precious metal proofs only (see page 180). This is the first to be sold cheaply in BU-pack format. Various other versions in silver and gold with various face values were sold, up to the £1,000 coin!

COMMEMORATIVE TYPE WORDSWORTH

Standard Fifth portrait of QEII
Design by: Jody Clark
Scene with name and years of birth and death.
Design by: David Lawrence
Edge: (on proofs)
I WANDERED LONELY AS A CLOUD

		BU	Proof
2020	(all originally sold in folders)	£13.00	
3,000 max	.925 sterling silver proof, price new		£82.50
?	.925 sterling silver piedfort proof, price new		?
300 max	.917 gold proof, price new		£2495.00

A piedfort proof version doesn't seem to exist.

COMMEMORATIVE TYPE
TOWER 2020 1 (of 4)
Standard Fifth portrait of QEII
Design by: Jody Clark
The White Tower
Design by: Timothy Noad
Edge: Milled (precious metal
versions not yet known)

		BU	Proof
2020	(all originally sold in folders)	£13.00	
2,500 max	.925 sterling silver proof, price new		£82.50
450 max	.925 sterling silver piedfort proof, price new		£155.00
125 max	.917 gold proof, price new		£2495.00

Coins 2 - 4 of the series are planned for August, October and November.

COMMEMORATIVE TYPE
MUSIC LEGENDS 1 (of ?)
Standard Fifth portrait of QEII
Design by: Jody Clark
The Band Queen (instruments)
Design by: Chris Facey
Edge: (on the 1oz silver proof):
Mercury, Taylor, Deacon and May

		BU	Proof
2020	(all originally sold in folders)*	£13.00	
17,500 max	Silver 1/2oz (£1) proof, price new		£60.00
7,500 max	Silver 1oz (£2) proof, with gold detail, price new		£90.00
500 max	Silver 2oz (£5) proof, price new		£180.00
1,250 max	Gold 1/4oz (£25) proof, price new		£510.00
300 max	Gold 1oz (£100) proof, price new		£2,195.00

*In addition to the standard BU folder, three other BU folders were sold for £15 each, featuring the artwork of the albums 'Hot Space', 'Live', and 'A Kind of Magic'.

Note that the precious metal versions all have different marked face values and that the two smallest silver coins have lower face values than their cupro-nickel BU counterpart!

COMMEMORATIVE TYPE
JAMES BOND 1 (of 3)
Standard Fifth portrait of QEII
Design by: Jody Clark
Aston Martin DB5
Design by: Matt Dent and
Christian Davies
Edge: Milled on all versions

		BU	Proof
2020	(all originally sold in folders)	£13.00	
15,007 max	Silver 1/2oz (£1) proof, price new		£65.00
7,007 max	Silver 1oz (£2) proof, price new		£88.00
2,007 max	Silver 2oz (£5) proof, price new		£235.00
1,007 max	Gold 1/4oz (£25) proof, price new		£555.00
350 max	Gold 1oz (£100) proof, price new		£2,250.00
250 max	Gold 2oz (£200) proof, price new		£4,310.00

Note that the precious metal versions all have different marked face values and that the two smallest silver coins have lower face values than their cupro-nickel BU counterpart!

FORTHCOMING IN 2020
Also planned for paced 2020 release are a further two James Bond coins (one showing the Lotus Esprit and the other a tuxedo), another three Tower of London themed coins, an Elton John coin as part of the Music Legends series and also coins for the 15th anniversary of the British Red Cross and one to mark seventy-five years since the end of WWII.

Twenty Pound coins ave been sold new by the Royal Mint since 2013, for £20.00 plus postage. The value of the silver content is about £6.30. The coins are not accepted in shops or at any banks or post offices. See also £50 coin on the next pages.

OBVERSE 1
Coins 1 - 3

OBVERSE 2, Coins
4 - 8, 10 & 11

5

6, 8, 10 & 11

Above: 9
(both sides)

1

3

2

4

7

* Prices quoted are for coins in original packets.

2013	Coin 1: St. George reverse, 250,000 sold	£16 - £20*
2014	Coin 2: WWI 1914 1918 Britannia reverse	£16 - £20*
2015	Coin 3: Winston Churchill reverse	£16 - £22*
2015	Coin 4: Longest Reign reverse	£18 - £22*
2016	Coin 5: Queen's 90th reverse, 116,354 sold	£17 - £22*
2016	Coin 6: Welsh Dragon reverse (see note, below)	£28.00*
2016	Coin 7: Christmas Nativity scene, 29,929 sold	£24 - £30*
2017	Coin 8: Welsh Dragon (as Coin 6, dated 2017)	£24 - £27*
2017	Coin 9: Royal Wedding, same design as £5, type 45	£17 - £20*
2018	Coin 10: Welsh Dragon (as Coin 6, dated 2018)	£27.00*
2019	Coin 11: Welsh Dragon (as Coin 6, dated 2019)	£27.00*
2020	Coin 12: Welsh Dragon (as Coin 6, dated 2020)	£27.00*

The design used on the 2015 Longest Reign coin was also used for a 5oz silver proof (£395.00 price new, 65mm diameter), 1 kilo silver proof (£2000.00 price new, 100mm) and 1 kilo gold proof coins (price new £42,500.00). The 2016 Welsh Dragon coins were sold at the Royal Mint visitor centre in special packaging and later in different, standard packaging. On the Welsh dragon coins the 'TWENTY POUNDS' is incorporated under the dragon and is therefore not included in the wording around the Queen.

155

The £50 Coin

Clearly the £20 coin was quite successful for the Royal Mint Ltd, so the marketing department introduced the short-lived £50 coins (and a £100 coin, on the next page). The current bullion value is about £11.97.

A few years ago a gentleman attempted to pay a total of £29,300 worth of Royal Mint £100 coins in to his bank account. The bank appear to have contacted the mint, who it seems were getting more of them back than they cared to receive (and once they are out of their packets and have scratches and scrapes they can't sell them again, but still have to recompense the banks), so they issued a memo to the Post Office and to some banks (possibly all banks) in January 2016 telling them not to accept the high value silver (£20, £50 and £100) coins at face value. I warned about a similar potential scenario when the first £20 coin was issued in 2013.

A Royal Mint spokesman says that 'Legal tender allows UK coins to be accepted for payment of debts in court, but only circulating legal tender coins (i.e. the conventional £2 coin and lower values) are designed to be spent and traded at businesses and banks.'

So there is a two-tier legal tender system of circulating coins and non-circulating coins that are legal tender, but aren't really? As far as I'm concerned, with no acceptance at any banks, these coins are all worth whatever the market is willing to pay for them. These were discontinued after 2016, and rightly so!

                Britannia Coin   **Reverse of Shakespeare Coin**

		BU
2015	£50 Britannia with lion, in package	£30-£50
2016	£50 Shakespeare theme, in package (14,948 sold)	£40-£60
	Obverse has: ELIZABETH II DG REG FD 50 POUNDS	

The £100 Coin

The Royal Mint made and sold its first £100 coin in 2015. 50,000 of them were sold for £100 each. Currently the silver value is about £25.14 and again, I'm not entirely clear on the true legal tender status of these coins (they seem to only be worth £100 when the owner and any potential buyers believe they are, as long as they don't actually try to spend one! See also notes for the silver £20 and £50 coins). Late 2015 saw the issue of another £100 coin with the new portrait of the Queen and featuring Buckingham palace on its reverse. The 2016 £100 coin featured Trafalgar Square with the lion in the foreground and Nelson's column in the background. Incidentally, the three designs used to for the £100 coins were also used for three coins of the 'Portrait of Britain (2014 and 2016)' series of £5 crown coins. In crown guise they were Tri-Chromatic pad coloured.

The Royal Mint seem to have given up on them now, so I can only assume sales slumped drastically following the revelations that they weren't actually worth what is written on them.

The first £100 Coin (2015)

Standard portrait of Queen Elizabeth II. Design by: Ian Rank-Broadley
The Elizabeth Tower as seen from below. Design by: Glyn Davies and Laura Clancy

The second £100 Coin (2015)

New portrait of QEII with '100 POUNDS 2015'. Design by: Jody Clark
Buckingham Palace with Queen Victoria monument. Design by:
Glyn Davies and Laura Clancy

40 mm • 62.86 grammes • .999 Silver • edge: milled

The third and last £100 Coin (2016), Not Illustrated
Portrait of QEII with '100 POUNDS 2015'. Design by: Jody Clark
Trafalgar Square. Design by: Glyn Davies and Laura Clancy

			BU
2015	50,000 max	'Big Ben' tower, specimen in folder	£70-£100
2015	50,000 max	Buckingham Palace, specimen in folder	£70-£100
2016	45,000 max	Trafalgar Square, specimen in folder (14,878 sold)	£75-£100

19.41 mm • 3.35 grammes • .925 Silver • edge: milled

The Sixpence
Originally a popular 'old school' coin, first made in 1551 as it was conveniently 1/40th of a Pound and people actually used to spend them, until their demonetisation in 1980 (nearly all coins were made with the sole intention of being spent in those days - crazy isn't it)! It was re-introduced in 2016 to the same size, weight and silver fineness as the pre 1920 sixpences but is now revalued as six new pence instead of six old pence (which is 2.5p in new pence).

I assume these are aimed at the wedding industry - 'something old, something new and a sixpence in her shoe'? Delightful older sixpence coins in perfect condition are often cheaper and readily available from reputable coin dealers, albeit without the fancy paperwork or bulky packaging, which I imagine must be quite uncomfortable when worn in a shoe.

Right now they are available new for £30.00, in a wedding presentation style box. They did used to be available for £15 in a card pack. The obverse type is the same as the 2015 Britannia £50 coin.

New sixpences have so far been struck dated 2016, 2017, 2018, 2019 and 2020.

Sixpence -
actual size

Sixpence -
enlarged

United Kingdom Banknotes

The UK currently has four denominations of legal tender banknotes in circulation; the £5, £10, £20 and £50 notes. Some banks in Scotland and in Northern Ireland also issue Sterling banknotes in the same denomination as the Bank of England types (plus the Royal Bank of Scotland continues to issue smaller numbers of £1 notes). These notes are not officially legal tender but they are of course readily accepted within the countries in which they circulate. All of the Scottish and Northern Irish banknotes have to be backed up by Bank of England money; in other words, a bank issuing notes in Scotland or Northern Ireland has to theoretically hold in its vaults the same amount of Bank of England money. Usually this Bank of England money is held in the form of special high-value banknotes that are exchanged just between banks. The circulating Scottish and Northern Ireland banknotes are not covered in this book.

The five current circulating Bank of England notes are: <u>Polymer £5</u> - Mainly green with Winston Churchill on the reverse, <u>polymer £10</u> - Mainly orange with Jane Austen on the reverse, <u>paper £20</u> - Mainly purple with Adam Smith on the reverse and <u>paper £50</u> - Mainly red with Matthew Boulton and James Watt on the reverse.

The 'promise to pay the bearer' on each Bank of England banknote never expires, even when notes of that type have long since been removed from circulation. As a result, every single Bank of England note can always be redeemed for its face value at the Bank of England, and usually at any UK bank. Shopkeepers and other merchants are not obliged to accept older Bank of England notes. Before redeeming older Bank of England notes it's obviously a good idea to check that they don't have a collectable value first.

Banknote condition

Just as with coins, condition plays a very important role where the values of banknotes are concerned. Most collectors will attempt to collect banknotes in the best condition they can afford. With modern banknotes this will nearly always be uncirculated (mint condition) examples, as such examples of modern banknotes are usually obtainable. With this in mind, most well-used, tatty, creased and dirty banknotes that have exchanged hands many times are only likely to be worth their face value. EF is an abbreviation for Extremely Fine and means that a note is in very good condition, but just a little way from being classed as UNCirculated. VF means Very Fine and is quite a common grade for modern notes that have seen average use.

Serial numbers

Collectors like interesting serial numbers too. If you ever get given a note with a low serial number, where at least the first 3 digits of the 6 digit number are zeros, keep hold of it. A note with the serial number AH43 000954 will be slightly more interesting than AH43 874563, for example. The note AH43 000001 would of course be more interesting, still. AA01 000045 would be even more desirable! Collectors also like interesting patterns in numbers, like AH43 434343, AH22 222222 or AH12 345678. You won't get offered huge amounts of money for notes with interesting serial numbers, but you might persuade someone to give you more than face value, assuming the note is in good condition.

The new polymer £5 note. The red area
shows the transparent window.

DETAILS   **UNC**

The Bank of England are moving from paper notes to polymer (plastic). Polymer notes are harder wearing and harder to fake. The first polymer note, the new £5, was released into circulation on the 13th September 2016. The new notes circulated along-side the existing paper £5 notes until the old notes were completely removed from circulation in May 2017.

Signed by <u>Victoria Cleland</u>, chief cashier of the Bank of England from March 2014 to June 2018

Letter, Letter, Number, Number, followed by 6 digits

AA01 followed by 6 digits (first polymer £5 note prefix) -	
Lower than 000500 serial number	£1,000+
Lower than 100000	£15 - £100
Higher than 100000	£5 - £10
Other prefixes (in as-new condition)	up to £10

As seems to be the norm these days when a new coin or bank note is introduced, there was silliness on eBay, especially regarding AA01 and AK47 notes. Quite how many of the eBay sales were to genuine buyers is another matter, but prices initially went wild nonetheless. The media picked up on it and added further fuel. After a few weeks it all came crashing down, as usual, and prices have been fairly stable since then.

Banknote images are © Bank of England.

The new polymer £10 note. The dark red
area shows the transparent window.

DETAILS   UNC

The polymer £10 was introduced on the 14th September 2017 and circulated along-side the old paper note until March 2018.

Signed by <u>Victoria Cleland</u>, chief cashier of the Bank of England from March 2014 to June 2018.

Letter, Letter, Number, Number, followed by 6 digits

AA01 followed by 6 digits (first polymer £10 note prefix) -	
Lower than 000500 serial number	£1,000+
Lower than 100000	£30 - £100
Higher than 100000	£20 - £30
Other prefixes (in as-new condition). Last prefixes were AM, BM, CM, DM	up to £15

Signed by <u>Sarah John</u>, chief cashier of the Bank of England from June 2018 onwards.

DJxx followed by 6 digits (first known John prefix) -	£20
Other prefixes (in as-new condition)	up to £15

COLLECTORS' COINS - DECIMAL ISSUES OF THE UK

Banknote images are © Bank of England.

The old paper £20 is currently circulating in parallel with the new (introduced 20/2/20) polymer note. The old paper £20 can be used until further notice.

DETAILS	EF	UNC

Signed by <u>Andrew Bailey</u>, the chief cashier of the Bank of England from 2004 to 2011.

Letter, Letter, Number, Number, followed by 6 digits

	EF	UNC
AA01 followed by 6 digits (first Bailey prefix)	£50.00	£200.00*
AA** followed by 6 digits (first Bailey prefix)	£25.00	£38.00
AL** followed by 6 digits (special column sort prefix)	£25.00	£38.00
LL** followed by 6 digits (replacement notes)	£30.00	£50.00
HD36 followed by 6 digits (last Bailey prefix)		£38.00

* Very low serial numbers will be worth more.

Signed by <u>Chris Salmon</u> the chief cashier of the Bank of England from 2011 to March 2014.

Letter, Letter, Number, Number, followed by 6 digits

HA** followed by 6 digits (first Salmon prefix)	£30.00
Mid Salmon prefixes	£26.00
JH** followed by 6 digits (last Salmon prefix)	£30.00

Signed by <u>Victoria Cleland</u>, chief cashier of the Bank of England from March 2014 to June 2018.

Letter, Letter, Number, Number, followed by 6 digits

JH** followed by 6 digits (first Cleland prefix)	£35.00
Later Cleland prefixes	£28.00

The new polymer £20 note, Signed by <u>Sarah John</u>, the chief cashier from June 2018 to date.

The dark red areas show the transparent windows.

Letter, Letter, Number, Number, followed by 6 digits

AA01 followed by 6 digits (first polymer £20 prefix)	£35.00
Other prefixes	£28.00

Very low AA01 serial numbers will attract a premium. Expect the usual nonsense on eBay!

Banknote images are © Bank of England.

DETAILS   UNC

Signed by <u>Chris Salmon</u>, the chief cashier of the Bank of England from 2011 to March 2014.

Letter, Number, Number, followed by 6 digits

AA** followed by 6 digits (first prefix)	£85.00*
Mid Salmon prefixes	£75.00
AJ** followed by 6 digits (last prefix)	£85.00

*Very low AA01 notes are worth more.

Signed by <u>Victoria Cleland</u>, chief cashier of the Bank of England from March 2014 to June 2018.

Letter, Number, Number, followed by 6 digits

AJ** followed by 6 digits (first prefix)	£85.00
Later Cleland prefixes (noted to AK**)	£75.00

Chief Cashier Signatures on Current Bank of England notes

Dr Andrew John Bailey,
Chief Cashier 2004 - 2011
(his signature can be seen on some paper
£20 notes)

Chris Salmon, Chief Cashier 2011 - 2014
(his signature can be seen on some paper
£20 and £50 notes)

Victoria Cleland, Chief Cashier 2014 to
June 2018 (her signature can currently be
seen on the polymer £5, some £10 notes,
and also on the newest paper £20 and £50
notes)

Sarah John, Chief Cashier 2018 - date
(her signature can be seen on the new
polymer £20 notes and on some polymer
£10 notes)

Introduced as a special optional feature of the Royal Mint Experience tour, the 'Strike Your Own' coins are inexpensive to buy from the source and have proved popular. The exclusivity of the packaging, in that you physically have to be at the Royal Mint premises to get one (even though most of the coins themselves were also made available in some other form of packaging) has caused the odd SYO coin to go a bit potty on eBay, due in part to social media influence. For certain coins, people have travelled to the Royal Mint and gone on many tours over many days and have taken other measures, just to get as many 'Strike Your Own' coins as possible to put straight on to eBay, in order to ride the wave of hype that annoyingly seems to accompany almost every new coin issue these days! These pages show the standard* SYO coin range so far, with their current market values and other details.

Rumour has it that SYO coins are not quite to the Royal Mint 'Brilliant Uncirculated' standard, as they are not always struck as many times as BU coins. The gate-fold coin cards include some other basic information. The coins themselves are gripped in a plastic holder with a gap at the top to facilitate removal. The cards measure 12x7cm (with the exception of coin 1, which is 12x7.3cm).

1. 2016 Last Round £1, 18/5/2016 to 31/12/2016. Heraldic beasts design. None of these coins were made for circulation but they were available in other packs/sets.

2. 2017 New 12-sided £1, 1/1/2017 to 16/10/2017. Nations of the Crown design. These coins were available in other packs/sets and were also circulated (in standard quality).

3. 2017 Isaac Newton 50p, 17/10/2017 to 31/12/2017.
4. 2018 Isaac Newton 50p, 1/1/2018 to 18/3/2018. The 2017 coins were available in other packs/sets and were also circulated (in standard quality). 2018 dated Newton coins were exclusively made available as SYO coins - and as the Royal Mint re-used the cards, they are seen with either 2017 or 2018 printed dates on the back.

5. 2018 Britannia £2, 19/3/2018 to 31/9/2018. None of these coins were made for circulation but were available in annual BU sets.

*Silver and Gold VIP tour participants can, at a cost of £125.00, strike a silver proof coin which is provided with a COA personally signed by the Queen's assay master.

7. 2018 Frankenstein £2, 1/10/2018 to 18/11/2018.
None of these coins were made for circulation but were available in other packs/sets.

Christmas Nutcracker 2018 £5

8. 2018 Nutcracker £5, 19/11/2018 to 31/12/2018.
The Christmas Nutcracker SYO was provided in a plastic capsule, in the same type of drawstring bag as above right, accompanied by a 5x5cm printed card. None of these coins were made for circulation but were available in other packs.

10. 2019 Britannia £2, 1/4/2019 to 27/6/2019.
Same as No. 5, shown on the previous page. None of these coins were made for circulation but were available in annual BU sets.

6. 2018 Royal Wedding £5, 19 & 20th May 2018.
In a departure from the normal coin-on-a-card format, the Royal Wedding SYO was provided in a plastic capsule, in a drawstring bag accompanied by a 5x5cm printed card. None of these coins were made for circulation but were available in other packs.

9. 2019 NEW PENCE 50p, 1/1/2019 to 31/3/2019.
The first SYO of 2019 is the 'NEW PENCE' 50p - the reverse design that was originally used 1969-1981 combined with a 2019 obverse. This coin is also included in proof/silver proof form in special 2019 sets of 50p coins (and may also appear in a BU set).

11. 2019 Conan Doyle 50p, 28/6/2019 to 23/9/2019.
This coin was also included in annual sets and individual BU packs.

167

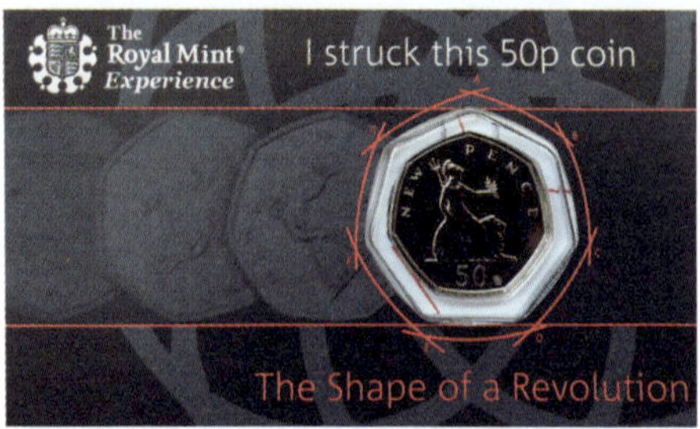

12. 2019 50p with mint mark, 24/9/2019 to 28/10/2019.
This coin was also sold in individual BU packs.

14. 2019 Snowman & Boy 50p, 1/12/2019 to 31/12/2019.
This was the second Snowman themed coin - the first was never offered in SYO guise. This coin was also available in individual BU packs.

15. 2019 Britannia £2, 1/1/2020 to 30/1/2020.
Same as No. 5, shown on the previous page spread. None of these coins were made for circulation but were available in annual BU sets.

Note, I have included a sales figures on the next page for SYO products, where known.

13. 2019 Wallace & Gromit 50p, 29/10/2019 to 30/11/2019.
This coin was also sold in individual BU packs.

16. 2020 Brexit on the day, 31/1/2020.
This coin was also sold in individual BU packs and was also circulated in large numbers (in normal circulation quality)

17. 2020 Brexit 50p, 1/2/2020 to 12/2/2020.
For Brexit coins not struck on the day the packaging was very similar (not illustrated) - on the front both references to the 31 January 2020 are omitted and the 'I struck this 50p coin ' has been moved down a line and is also yellow in colour to match the 'A VOTE TO LEAVE AND A NEW ERA' text above the coin.

18. 2020 Megalosaurus 50p, 13/2/2020 to 15/3/2020. This coin was also sold in individual BU packs.

19. 2020 Iguanodon 50p, 16/3/2020 to 17/3/2020. This coin was also sold in individual BU packs.

Strike Your Own (SYO) Coins

2016	39,431	Coin 1, The Last Round Pound	£35
2017		Coin 2, The New Pound	£30
2017		Coin 3, Isaac Newton 50p (dated 2017)	£30
2018	19,934	Coin 4, Isaac Newton 50p (dated 2018, exclusively SYO)	£30
2018		Coin 5, Britannia £2	£35
2018	519	Coin 6, Harry & Meghan £5 (struck on 19 & 20/5/18)	£100-£160*
2018		Coin 7, Frankenstein £2	£22
2018		Coin 8, Nutcracker Christmas £5	£40
2019		Coin 9, NEW PENCE Fifty Pence (exclusively SYO)	£8
2019		Coin 10, Britannia £2	£22
2019		Coin 11, Conan Doyle (Sherlock Holmes) 50p	£30
2019		Coin 12, NEW PENCE 50p with mint-mark	£30
2019		Coin 13, Wallace & Gromit 50p	£25
2019		Coin 14, Snowman & Boy 50p	£25
2020		Coin 15, Britannia £2	£25
2020		Coin 16, Brexit 50p, struck on the day	£30
2020		Coin 17, Brexit 50p	£28
2020		Coin 18, Megalosaurus 50p	£25
2020		Coin 19, Iguanodon 50p**	£80

* Prices volatile as not often offered for sale. At least one fake card has been seen.
** Prices also volatile. The Iguanodon SYO was struck for two days only, before the Royal Mint closed to the public due to the novel corona virus pandemic.

From 1971 to 1982, The Royal Mint issued proof coin sets sealed in plastic, enclosed in lightweight card envelopes. The coins within often tone badly over time and the card outer case is sometimes worse for wear. Values at the upper end of the ranges shown below are usually for sets in very good condition. Values fluctuate and sets can often be purchased for less and sometimes they sell for more, especially as gifts for round birthday's, so expect 1978, 1988 and 1998 to potentially climb in value a little during 2018.

Year	No. of Coins.	Price New*	Notes	Value
1971	6	£3.15		£6 - £12
1972	7	£3.25	Inc. Crown	£13 - £20
1973	6	£5.90*		£8 - £12
1974	6	£5.90*		£8 - £12
1975	6	£5.90*		£8 - £12
1976	6	£5.90*		£8 - £12
1977	7	£8.30*	Inc. Crown	£8 - £12
1978	6	£6.40*		£8 - £12
1979	6	£6.40*		£8 - £12
1980	6	£9.00		£8 - £10
1981	6	£9.95		£8 - £12
1982	7	£11.95	20p added	£8 - £12

In 1983, the packaging was changed to a blue leatherette bookshelf type case.

Year	No. of Coins.	Price New*	Notes	Value
1983	8	£17.25	£1 added	£10 - £15
1984	8	£17.95		£10 - £15

From 1985 onward, two types of packaging were offered: The "standard" blue leatherette case, and the "deluxe" red leather case. Values don't tend to be vastly different.

Year	No. of Coins.	Price New*	Notes	Value
1985	7	£18.75 blue / £25.75 red		£10 - £15
1986	8	£21.25 blue / £28.25 red	Inc. commem. £2	£10 - £15
1987	7	£18.95 blue / £25.95 red		£10 - £15
1988	7	£18.95 blue / £25.95 red		£15 - £20
1989	9	£22.95 blue / £29.95 red	Inc. both £2	£35 - £50
1990	8	£21.95 blue / £29.95 red		£12 - £20
1991	7	£22.95 blue / £29.95 red		£12 - £20
1992	9	£27.50 blue / £34.50 red	2x 10p, 2x 50p	£50 - £65
1993	8	£28.75 blue / £35.50 red	Inc. Crown	£15 - £20
1994	8	£24.75 blue / £32.50 red	Inc. commem £2	£15 - £20
1995	8	£26.65 blue / £34.50 red		£15 - £20
1996	9	£29.75 blue / £37.50 red		£20 - £30
1997	10	£32.50 blue / £39.50 red		£20 - £30
1998	10	£32.95 blue / £39.95 red		£30 - £50
1999	9	£33.95 blue / £39.95 red		£40 - £50
2000	10	£29.95 std / £39.95 special		£20 - £30

* The prices marked with an asterisk are what the sets were originally sold for in the USA, converted to GBP at the then exchange rate - source 'Standard Catalog of World Coins' published by KP books. Contact me if you have original printed material showing the UK retail prices for the 1973 - 1979 sets.

From 2001 on, it is accepted that all sets will contain the standard 8 pieces: 1p, 2p, 5p, 10p, 20p, 50p, £1, and £2. The Royal Mint, also produced deluxe proof sets and executive proof sets, which all contain the same coins but have better packaging. The deluxe and executive sets are sometimes sold for up to 20% more than the standard sets.

Sets that include currently higher priced coins (e.g. the 2009 set containing the Kew Gardens 50p) are priced higher than others, which is a little odd really, as the numbers of proof sets (and therefore proof coins) made is generally around the same - approximately 35,000 sets were sold in 2009, which is about the same as the number of sets sold in 2008, but just because the 2008 set doesn't include a 'special' coin, it's currently worth well over £100 less! Proof coins are of course very different to their normal circulation counterparts, but in general they don't seem to be viewed as different types of coins by the public, but rather as higher quality versions of the normal coins.

Recently 'Premium' sets have been introduced which include a medallion. In 2013 the Royal Mint made the proof sets available in reduced size 'definitive' form, which include just the standard 1p to £2, a 'commemorative' set which is just the commemorative 50p, £1, £2 and £5 coins and also a complete set (named a 'Collector set') made up of all the coins. I'm starting to lose track, and I honestly don't think the packaging will play much of a roll in the future - the coins are what they are, regardless of the current sales/packaging strategy! Obviously the definitive and commemorative 'short' sets are worth less than the full sets. They now also sell silver proof sets of all of the annual coins, silver proof sets of just the commemorative coins, silver proof piedfort sets of just the commemorative coins and gold proof sets of just the commemorative coins!

If the various types of packaging, alloys and coin configurations weren't confusing enough, the annual proof sets no longer necessarily actually contain all of the coins from a given year. For example there are no sets that contain the 2015 5th portrait Battle of Britain 50p, 5th portrait 2015 Royal Navy £2 or 5th portrait 2015 Magna Carta £2. Also, the 2016 and 2017 proof sets contain none of the Beatrix Potter 50p coins.

Year	No. of Coins.	Price New (deluxe to 2011)	Value
2001	10	£39.50	£20 - £30
2002	9	£45.50	£20 - £30
2003	11	£46.50	£20 - £30
2004	10	£39.95	£20 - £30
2005	12	£48.50	£40 - £50
2006	13	£49.95	£40 - £50
2007	12	£49.95	£40 - £50
2008	11	£49.95	£40 - £50
2009	12	£49.99	£200 - £250
2010	13	£49.99	£50 - £60
2011	14	£51.25	£180 - £200
2012	10	£75.00 "Collector set"	£60 - £90
2013	15	£110.00 "Collector set"	£130 - £150
2014	14	£110.00 "Collector set"	£170 - £200
2015	13	£110.00 "Collector set"	£100 - £130
2016 (6,919 sold)	16	£145.00 "Collector set"	£170 - £200
2017 & 2018	13	£145.00 "Collector set"	£170-£200
2019 & 2020		£155.00"Collector set", price new	

171

1982 Proof set, resting on it's card outer and certificate
- pre 1980 sets did not include a certificate.

1985 Proof set in standard blue leatherette, from
above with certificate. The blue and red mid 1980s
to late 1990s cases can also be opened like this to
aid display.

1988 Deluxe Proof set in red leather case.

2003 Standard Proof set in red box - early 2000s standard sets were sold in either blue or red boxes like this.

In 1982, the Royal Mint introduced Brilliant Uncirculated sets, which contain most of the coins contained in the Proof sets (crowns normally not included). These sets do not have proof-quality striking, and are packaged in a folder style with text to provide historic background information and specifications of the coins.

Year	Pieces	Coins	Notes
1982	7	$\frac{1}{2}$p, 1p, 2p, 5p, 10p, 20p, 50p	
1983	8	$\frac{1}{2}$p, 1p, 2p, 5p, 10p, 20p, 50p, £1	new £1 added
1984	8	$\frac{1}{2}$p, 1p, 2p, 5p, 10p, 20p, 50p, £1	
1985	7	1p, 2p, 5p, 10p, 20p, 50p, £1	$\frac{1}{2}$p removed
1986	8	1p, 2p, 5p, 10p, 20p, 50p, £1, £2	Commonwealth Games
1987	7	1p, 2p, 5p, 10p, 20p, 50p, £1	
1988	7	1p, 2p, 5p, 10p, 20p, 50p, £1	
1989	7	1p, 2p, 5p, 10p, 20p, 50p, £1	
1990	8	1p, 2p, 5p, 5p, 10p, 20p, 50p, £1	Large & small 5p
1991	7	1p, 2p, 5p, 10p, 20p, 50p, £1	
1992	9	1p, 2p, 5p, 10p, 10p, 20p, 50p, 50p, £1	lg & sm 10p; EEC 50p
1993	8	1p, 2p, 5p, 10p, 20p, 50p, £1, £5	Coronation Anniversary
1994	8	1p, 2p, 5p, 10p, 20p, 50p, £1, £2	Bank of England
1995	8	1p, 2p, 5p, 10p, 20p, 50p, £1, £2	Dove of Peace
1996	8	1p, 2p, 5p, 10p, 20p, 50p, £1, £2	Football
1997	9	1p, 2p, 5p, 10p, 20p, 50p, 50p, £1, £2	Large & small 50p
1998	9	1p, 2p, 5p, 10p, 20p, 50p, 50p, £1, £2	EU
1999	8	1p, 2p, 5p, 10p, 20p, 50p, £1, £2	Rugby £2 (no normal £2)
2000	9	1p, 2p, 5p, 10p, 20p, 50p, 50p, £1, £2	Public Libraries
2001	9	1p, 2p, 5p, 10p, 20p, 50p, £1, £2, £2	Marconi
2002	8	1p, 2p, 5p, 10p, 20p, 50p, £1, £2	
2003	10	1p, 2p, 5p, 10p, 20p, 50p, 50p, £1, £2, £2	Women's Suffrage, DNA
2004	10	1p, 2p, 5p, 10p, 20p, 50p, 50p, £1, £2, £2	Bannister, Trevithick
2005	10	1p, 2p, 5p, 10p, 20p, 50p, 50p, £1, £2, £2	Dictionary, Guy Fawkes
2006	10	1p, 2p, 5p, 10p, 20p, 50p, 50p, £1, £2, £2	Victoria Cross, Brunel
2007	9	1p, 2p, 5p, 10p, 20p, 50p, £1, £2, £2	Slave trade, Act of Union
2008	7	1p - £1 old designs 'Emblems of Britain'	
2008	7	1p - £1 new designs	
2008	14	1p - £1 both designs	
2008	9	1p, 2p, 5p, 10p, 20p, 50p, £1, £2, £2	Old designs. Olympic £2.
2009	11	1p, 2p, 5p, 10p, 20p, 50p, 50p, £1, £2, £2, £2	Kew, Burns, Darwin.
2010	8	1p, 2p, 5p, 10,p 20p, 50p, £1, £2	
2011	13	1p, 2p, 5p, 10p, 20p, 50p, 50p, £1 x3, £2 x3	

Year	Pieces	Coins	Notes
2011	13	1p, 2p, 5p, 10p, 20p, 50p, 50p, £1 x3, £2 x3	
2012	10	1p, 2p, 5p, 10p, 20p, 50p, £1, £2, £2, £5	
2013	15	1p, 2p, 5p, 10p, 20p, 50p x2, £1 x3, £2 x4, £5	
2014	14	1p, 2p, 5p, 10p, 20p, 50p x2, £1 x3, £2 x3, £5	
2015	13	1p, 2p, 5p, 10p, 20p, 50p x2, £1, £2 x3, £5 x2	
2016	16	1p, 2p, 5p, 10p, 20p, 50p x2, £1 x2, £2 x6, £5	£55 price new
2017/18	13	1p,.2p, 5p, 10p, 20p, 50p x2, £1, £2 x3, £5 x2	£55 price new
2019/20			£55 price new

The BU sets tend to sell from between 2.5x to 5x the face value of the coins included. Sets in mint condition with absolutely no toning on any of the coins will attract a premium. Some sets are affected by the current higher prices of some of the coins contained within, for example the 2009 set is affected by the current value of the Kew Gardens 50p. See 50p Commemorative Type 13 for further details. 106,332 of the 2009 set were sold.

Recently BU sets of 'definitive' coins have also been sold, which just contain the standard 1p to £2 coins and no commemoratives. Over the years there have also been other packaging options included a baby theme and wedding theme.

The sets below were specially marketed for commemorative or promotional purposes. Other later sets exist and may be included in a future edition. To be honest though, they aren't really incredibly popular and the total value is usually based strongly on the sum of the value of the coins contained within.

1983	7	½p, 1p, 2p, 5p, 10p, 20p, 50p Specially packaged set for the H J Heinz Company.	
1983	8	½p, 1p, 2p, 5p, 10p, 20p, 50p, £1 Specially packaged set for the Martini & Rossi Company.	
1988	7	1p, 2p, 5p, 10p, 20p, 50p, £1 Special package celebrating Australia's Bicentennial.	
1996	14 (7+7)	1p, 2p, 5p, 10p, 20p, 50p, £1; pre-decimal 1/2d, 1d, 3d, 6d, 1/, 2/, 2/6d Special package commemorating 25 years of decimalisation.	
2000	9	1p,2p,5p,10p,20p,50p,£1,£2, £5 (Millennium) In special "Time Capsule" packaging.	
2004	3	50p (Roger Bannister), £1 (Forth bridge), £2 (Trevithick's Locomotive) "Celebrating Human Achievement"	
2005	3	50p (Johnson's dictionary), £1 (Menai bridge), £2 (Guy Fawkes) new packaging of commemorative issues	

The following are sterling (.925) silver proof sets, designed for various occasions, including the introduction of the coins themselves. These are normally found in hard acrylic capsules, enclosed in a clam-shell case, and with a certificate from the Royal Mint. Some issues post 1998 are included in the main section.

Please note that the coins and sets of coins on the following four pages are not necessarily exhaustive. The pairs and sets of coins in particular have been issued in an almost random fashion over the years and tend to have sold new in fairly low numbers. On the second hand market years later there are very few, if any, that are worth substantially more than the total value of the coins contained within.

Five Pence

1990	35,000	large & small sized pair	£25.00

Ten Pence

1992	35,000	large & small sized pair	£25.00

Fifty Pence

1997	10,304	large & small sized pair	£25.00
1998	22,078	NHS issue and EU issue pair	£55.00
1998		pair, EU silver proof & EU silver Piedfort	£70.00

One Pound

1983 - 88	1,000	set of 6 regional designs, Arms, Shield	£75.00
1984 - 87	50,000	set of 4 regional designs	£90.00
1994 - 97	25,000	set of 4 regional designs	£100.00
1999 - 2002	25,000	set of 4 regional designs	£100.00

Two Pounds

1989	25,000	Bill of Rights & Claim of Rights pair	£60.00
1997	40,000	new bi-metallic circulation issue	£20.00
1998	25,000	new portrait on the circulation issue	£20.00
1997/98		bi-metallic Maklouf & Rank-Broadley pair	£35.00

ALERT

It seems that official Royal Mint cases were once obtainable, and some sets were assembled on the secondary market, with the individual coins and accompanying certificates. Original RM-issued sets usually contain a single certificate, listing each coin in the set.

1981	5,000	set, all issues, 1/2p-50p in base metals, sterling 25p commemorative, 22k gold Sovereign & £5	£700.00
1981		pair, sterling 25p commemorative, 22k gold Sovereign	£250.00
1992	1,000	set, both lg and sm 10p, 50p EEC, and £1	£75.00
1993	1,000	set, 50p EEC, £1, and £5 Coronation commem.	£75.00
1994	2,000	set, 50p D-Day, £1, and £2 Bank of England	£70.00
1995	1,000	silver set, peace £2, UN £2 and £1 coin	£50.00
1996	1,000	silver set, £5, £2 and £1 coins	£50.00
1996		set, all issues, 1p-£1 (25th Anniversary of Decimalisation)	£70.00
	500	pair, 1996 70th Birthday crown & 1997 Royal Wedding Jubilee crown	£60.00
1997		set, 50p, £1, £2, £5 Wedding Jubilee, £2 Britannia	£120.00
1999		set, £5 Millennium, £2 Britannia	£40.00
1999		set, £2 Britannia, £10 stamp	
2000	13,180	set, 1p-£5 Millennium, plus Maundy set (13 pieces)	£200.00
2000		£5 Millennium, plus YR2000 serial numbered £20 note	
		pair, 2002 Silver Jubilee crown & 2003 Coronation Jubilee crown	£60.00
2004		pair, 2004 Entente Cordiale crown & French €1 1/2 commem.	£75.00
2004	750	set, 50p Bannister, £1 Forth Bridge, £2 Trevithick, £5 Entente Cordiale £2 Britannia.	£75.00
-		1999, 2001, 2002, 2003 £2 Britannia uncirculated.	£80.00
2005		Pair of silver proof £5 coins - Nelson and Trafalgar	£65.00
2008		Set of 14 £1 coins, all designs 1983 to 2008. All dated 2008 with gold plated details	£300.00
2015		Silver proof set of definitive coins with the new portrait of the Queen, price new	£240.00

The following set was struck in .917 (22K) gold.

2002	2,002	set, 1p-£5 Golden Jubilee, plus Maundy set (13 pieces)	no data

Values of later sets including various combinations of coins that the Royal Mint offer tend to be worth about the same as the sum of the individual coins they contain.

Piedforts are coins that are double the thickness and weight of the normal version, and are almost always struck in sterling (.925) silver. These are normally found in hard acrylic capsules, enclosed in a clam-shell case, and with a certificate from the Royal Mint.

Five Pence

1990	20,000	.925 sterling silver, small size Piedfort	£20.00

Ten Pence

1992		.925 sterling silver, small size Piedfort	£30.00

Twenty Pence

1982		.925 sterling silver, Piedfort	£30.00

Fifty Pence

1997	7,192	.925 sterling silver, small size Piedfort	£50.00
1998		EEC & NHS pair, Piedfort	£30.00
1992/3 & 1998		.925 sterling silver Piedfort of both EU related coins	£85.00

One Pound

1983 - 88	500	set of 6 regional designs, Arms, Shield, Piedfort	£250.00
1984 - 87	10,000	.925 sterling silver, proof set of 4 Piedfort	£175.00
1994 - 97		.925 sterling silver, proof set of 4 Piedfort	£190.00
1999-2002	10,000	.925 sterling silver, proof set of 4 Piedfort	£225.00
2004-2007	1,400	.925 sterling silver, proof set of 4 Piedfort	£200.00

Two Pounds

1989	10,000	Bill of Rights & Claim of Rights pair, Piedfort	£30.00
1997	10,000	.925 sterling silver, Piedfort	£55.00
1998	10,000	.925 sterling silver, Piedfort £55	
1997/98	.10,000	925 sterling silver, Piedfort (pair)	£125.00
1999	10,000	.925 sterling silver, proof Piedfort HOLOGRAM	£100.00

Five Pounds

2005		Nelson & Trafalgar pair, Piedfort	£125.00

Sets

2003		set, 50p WPSU, £1 Royal Arms, £2 DNA Piedfort	£60.00
2004	7500	set, 50p Bannister, £1 Forth Bridge, £2 Trevithick Piedfort	£150.00
2005		set, 50p Johnson's Dictionary, £1 Menai Bridge, £2 Gunpowder Plot, £2 World War II Piedfort	£150.00
2007		£5, both £2 coins, £1 and 50p Piedfort	£250.00
2008		2x £5 coins, £2 and £1 Piedfort	£250.00
2008		The 7 new Dent design coins as silver Piedforts	£350.00
2009		Piedfort gold proof set of 16x difference 50 pence's	£ EXPENSIVE
2010		£5, £2, both £1 coins and the 50p	£300.00

Sets

2010/2011	Capital cities 4x £1 set	£300.00
2013	4x £5 coins, each with different Queen portrait	£683.00 new price
2013	The 5 Commemorative coins + the 2 £1 coins	£560.00 new price
2013	Pair of London Underground £2 coins	£200.00 new price
2014	The 4 Commemorative coins + the 2 £1 coins	£575.00 new price
2015	The 5 Commemorative coins	£570.00 new price

Special Collector Issues (Patterns)

A trial bi-metallic piece was issued in 1994 (predecessor to the £2 bi-metallic). The obverse shows a cutty (ship), while the reverse carries the Maklouf portrait of QEII. The ring bears the legend "ROYAL MINT TRIAL PATTERN", and an edge legend of 'ANNO REGNIA XLVI, DECUS ET TUTAMEN". See the £2 section.

Pattern sets issued by the Royal Mint to preview the new issue of "Bridges" £1 coins. All of these coins carry the date of 2003, and rather than having a face value, they are labelled as "PATTERN".

2003	7,500	.925 sterling silver, 7,500 , proof set of 4	£80.00
	3,000	.917 gold proof set of 4	£1500.00

A continuation of the above set, this set shows the "Beasts" series, which was a runner-up in the design competition for the new £1 coinage. All of these coins carry the date of 2004, and rather than having a face value, they are labelled as "PATTERN". Issued, as listed, in both sterling (.925) silver, and 22k (.917) gold.

2004	5,000	.925 sterling silver, proof set of 4	£90.00
	2,250	.917 gold proof set of 4	£1500.00

Coverage for the bullion issues is deliberately 'bare bones' just in order to give you an idea on the vast range of bullion issues sold by the Royal Mint. There are a lot of them!

The silver Britannia issues began in 1997 with proof-only coins. Commencing in 1998, originally the Royal Mint followed a pattern of using the standard Standing Britannia for every other year (even years), while bringing out new unique designs for the odd years. These coins were struck in Britannia silver (.9584 fine) which I thought was the whole point - coins featuring Britannia made of Britannia standard silver. From 2013 onwards they were struck in .999 silver and the diameter was reduced from 40mm to 38.61mm. Also from 2013 the Royal Mint introduced privy marks (on the edge) and also larger 5oz silver coins, the latter are not included in this book. From 2016 the new Jody Clark bust replaced the Ian Rank-Broadley bust of the queen.

In 2014 the RM introduced the 'Lunar' bullion range of coins, in .999 silver and also in .9999 gold. According to the blurb, they: 'Celebrate Chinese and British heritage with a dynamic design'. The silver 1oz versions are also 38.61mm in diameter.

In 2016 the RM introduced another bullion range of coins called the Queen's Beasts. There are eight different sizes (combined across gold and silver issues), most are available in proof form and some are available as just 'bullion' issues. In 2017 they introduced bullion coins themed as 'Landmarks of Britain' (four different ones so far). It all seems rather complicated and they seem very much aimed at the bullion market and less so for coin collectors. I suspect they are made to compete with other international bullion coin Issues.

Bullion Silver (UNC) £2 issues

1998	88,909	Standing Britannia (Reverse 2)	£23.00
1999	69,394	Britannia in Chariot (Reverse 1)	£23.00
2000	81,301	Standing Britannia (Reverse 2)	£28.00
2001	44,816	Una & the Lion (Reverse 3)	£40.00
2002	48,215	Standing Britannia (Reverse 2)	£30.00
2003	73,271	Helmeted Britannia facing left (Reverse 4)	£28.00
2004	100,000	Standing Britannia (Reverse 2)	£30.00
2005	100,000	Britannia seated (Reverse 5)	£50.00
2006	100,000	Standing Britannia (Reverse 2)	£30.00
2007	100,000	Britannia seated (Reverse 6)	£40.00
2008	100,000	Standing Britannia (not illustrated)	£25.00
2009	100,000	Britannia in Chariot (Reverse 1)	£28.00
2010	126,367	Bust of Britannia in profile (not illustrated)	£20.00
2011	100,000	Seated Britannia (not illustrated)	£20.00
2012	100,000	Standing Britannia (Reverse 2)	£20.00
2013		Reverse 2 (exists with snake privy mark#)	£20.00
2014		Reverse 2 (exists with horse privy mark#)	£20.00
2014		Mule error, with Lunar coin obverse (missing edge dentils)*	£80.00
2015		Standing Britannia (Reverse 2)	£20.00
2015		As above, with privy mark#	Scarce
2016		Standing Britannia (Reverse 2)	£20.00

* Not Illustrated. # Snake mintage est. 300,000. Horse est. 1,000,000. Goat est. 200,000

Silver (PROOF) issues (Reverse types from 1998 - 2012 are the same as previous)

Year	Denom.	Mintage	Notes	Price
1997	£2	4,173	Britannia in Chariot (Reverse 1)	£130.00
	20p	8,686	Both with Raphael Maklouf Bust	£20.00
1998	£2	2,168		£70.00
	20p	2,724		£20.00
2001	£2	3,047		£60.00
	20p	826		£20.00
2003	£2	1,833		£60.00
	20p	1,003		£20.00
2004	£2	5,000		£120.00
2005	£2	2,500		£60.00
2006	£2	2,500	With gold plated details	£130.00
2007	£2	5,147		£60.00
2008	£2	2,500		£60.00
	20p	725		£30.00
2009	£2	6,784		£60.00
	£1	2,500		£30.00
	50p	2,500		£20.00
	20p	3,500		£20.00
2010	£2	6,539		£50.00
	£1	3,497		£20.00
	50p	3,497		£20.00
	20p	4,486		£20.00
2011	£2	4,973		£50.00
	£1	2,483		£20.00
	50p	2,483		£20.00
	20p	2,483		£20.00
2012	£2	2,937		£50.00
2013	£10	4,054	From here on, reverses are not the same as	£300.00+?
	£2	3,468	those used on the bullion series (not illustrated)	£70.00
	20p			£30.00
	10p			£20.00

Britannia
Reverse 1

Britannia
Reverse 2

Britannia
Reverse 3

181

2014	£10		(not illustrated) Price new	£300.00+?
	£2			£70.00
2015	£10	650 max	(not illustrated*) Price new	£395.00
	£2	3000 max		£75.00
2016	£10		(not illustrated) Price new	£300.00+?
	£2	4150 max		£85.00

Britannia - Obverse type
used 1998 - 2015

Britannia Reverse 4

Britannia Reverse 5

Britannia Reverse 6

The Lunar series 2014 Horse

Lunar series 2015 Sheep
(obverse as 2014 Horse coin)

The Lunar series 2016 Monkey

Special (PROOF) sets

1997	11,832	Set of 4 (£2, £1, 50p, 20p)	£140.00
1998	3,044	Set of 4 (£2, £1, 50p, 20p)	£140.00
2001	4,596	Set of 4 (£2, £1, 50p, 20p)	£130.00
2003	3,623	Set of 4 (£2, £1, 50p, 20p)	£130.00
2005	5,000	Set of 4 (£2, £1, 50p, 20p)	£140.00
2006	-	Set of 5x different £2 with gold plated details	£250.00
2007	2,500	Set of 4 (£2, £1, 50p, 20p)	£130.00
2007		Set of 6 different £1 proofs	£140.00
2008		Set of 4 (£2, £1, 50p, 20p)	£130.00
2009		Set of 4 (£2, £1, 50p, 20p)	£130.00
2010		Set of 4 (£2, £1, 50p, 20p)	£130.00
2011		Set of 4 (£2, £1, 50p, 20p)	£150.00
2012		Set of 4 (£2, £1, 50p, 20p)	£150.00
2013	Now in .999 silver	Set of 5 (£2, £1, 50p, 20p, 10p)	£150.00
		Pair of 20p and 10p	£37.50 new price
2014		Set of 5	£200.00
2015			

Platinum 2007 Coins were issued to mark the 20th Anniversary of the 'Britannia'

2007	£10		1/10 oz Platinum	£200.00
2007	£25		1/4 oz Platinum	£450.00
2007		250	Set of 4 Platinum coins	£3000.00

Lunar coins, proof issue prices (bullion versions tend to sell for about 2-2.5x bullion value)

2014	Horse design, 1 ounce proof .999 Silver see previous page for picture	£82..50
	Mule error,* with Britannia coin obverse (edge dentils present)	£80.00
	Horse, 5 ounce proof .999 silver	£300.00
	Horse, 1 ounce proof .9999 gold	£1500.00
2015	Sheep, 1 ounce proof .999 silver	£82.50
	Sheep, Tenth of an ounce proof .9999 gold	£200.00
	Sheep, 1 ounce proof .999 silver (gold plated)	£110.00
	Sheep, 1 ounce proof .9999 gold	£1950.00
	Sheep, 5 ounce proof .999 silver	£350.00
	Sheep, 5 ounce proof .9999 gold	£7500.00
2016	Monkey, 1 ounce .999 silver	£82.50
	Monkey, Tenth of an ounce proof .9999 gold	£175.00
	Monkey, 1 ounce proof .9999 gold	£1450.00
	Monkey, 5 ounce proof .999 Silver	£395.00
	Monkey, 5 ounce proof .9999 gold	£7500.00
	Monkey, 1kg proof, .999 silver	£2000.00
	Monkey, 1kg proof, .9999 gold	£42,500.00

All 2014 - 2018 lunar reverse designs are by Wuon-Gean Ho. The 2017 lunar coins featured a rooster, 2018 was a dog, 2019 was a pig by Harry Brockway and for 2020 it was a rat by P J Lynch, which was also made available in base metal BU form.

* Est. mintage 33,000.

183

Gold Britannia issues began in 1987, as both bullion issues as well as proof issues. The values of the bullion issues are based on the value of the gold content, which fluctuates daily. The prices for these issues are given only as a guideline.

Bullion .917 Gold (UNC) Issues

£10	tenth ounce	Bullion Value + 30 to 50%
£25	quarter ounce	Bullion Value + 12 to 25%
£50	half ounce	Bullion Value + 8 to 20%
£100	one ounce	Bullion Value + 5 to 15%

The following are 4-piece sets, each coin encapsulated, and housed in a clamshell case,.

Special PROOF sets of 4 coins (for some dates, 3 or 5 coin sets were issued)

1987	10,000	Britannia standing	£2,700.00
1988	3,505	Britannia standing	£2,700.00
1989	2,268	Britannia standing	£2,700.00
1990	527	Britannia standing	£2,800.00
1991	509	Britannia standing	£2,800.00
1992	500	Britannia standing	£2,800.00
1993	462	Britannia standing	£2,800.00
1994	435	Britannia standing	£2,800.00
1995	500	Britannia standing	£2,800.00
1996	483	Britannia standing	£2,800.00
1997	892	Britannia standing	£2,800.00
1998	750	Britannia standing	£2,800.00
1999	750	Britannia standing	£2,800.00
2000	750	Britannia standing	£2,800.00
2001	1,000	Una & the Lion	£2,800.00
2002	945	Britannia standing	£2,800.00
2003	1,250	Britannia with Helmet	£2,800.00
2004	973	Britannia standing	£2,800.00
2005	1,439	Britannia seated	£2,800.00
2006	1,163	Britannia standing	£2,800.00
2007	1,250	Britannia seated	£2,800.00
2008	1,250	Britannia standing	£2,800.00
2009	797 max	Britannia standing in chariot	£2,800.00
2010	867 max	Britannia bust in profile	£2,800.00
2011	698 max	4 coin set	£2,800.00
		3 coin set	£1,900.00
2012	352	Britannia standing 4 coin set	£2,800.00
	99	3 coin set	no data
2013	261	Now .9999 gold	£2,900.00 new price
	136+90 premium	3 coin set	no data
2014		6 coin set	no data
		3 coin set	no data

2015	250 max	6 coin set	£2,895.00 new price
	250 max	3 coin set	£350.00 new price
2016	175 max	6 coin set	£3,175.00 new price
	70 max	3 coin premium set	£1,450.00 new price

Britannia (PROOF) individual cased coins

£100	1997	£1,800.00
£100	Other dates	£1,500.00-£1,700.00
£50	All dates	£700.00-£800.00
£25	All dates	£400.00-£450.00
£10	All dates	Around £180.00

Britannia (PROOF) platinum cased coins

£10	All dates	Around £200.00-£230.00
£25	2007 Noted	Around £400.00

Values of platinum Britannia coins tend to be as much as 4x the metal value. In comparison to the gold and silver issues, they are not often offered for sale.

The Queen's Beasts

In 2016 the Royal Mint introduced the Queen's Beasts series. There are eight different sizes (combined across gold and silver issues). This book aims to focus on actual coins, rather than the ever diversifying range of gold and silver coins that are not really coins at all in the strictest sense.

Gold Sovereign-based single coins are defined as non-commemorative Five Pounds, Two Pounds, Sovereigns and Half Sovereigns struck to normal or proof standards and sold singularly as gold bullion coins or as proof collectors' coins. The non-proof coins do not have boxes or certificates and are normally just traded as gold. Sovereigns and half sovereigns are 22 carat gold (.917 fine) and weigh 7.98g and 3.97g respectively.

Five Pounds

1984	Cased proof only	£1,800.00
1984	Cased proof only with 'U' in circle next to date	£1,700.00
1985	Cased proof only	£1,800.00
1985	with 'U' in circle next to date	£1,700.00
1986	with 'U' in circle next to date	£1,800.00
1987	with 'U' in circle next to date	£1,800.00
1988	with 'U' in circle next to date	£1,800.00
1989	Sovereign Anniversary type (on it's own, from a set)	£2,800.00
1989	Sovereign Anniversary type, cased proof	£3,200.00
1990	with 'U' in circle next to date	£1,800.00
1991	with 'U' in circle next to date	£1,800.00
1992	with 'U' in circle next to date	£1,800.00
1993	with 'U' in circle next to date	£1,800.00
1994	with 'U' in circle next to date	£1,800.00
1995	with 'U' in circle next to date	£1,800.00
1996	wIth 'U' in circle next to date	£1,800.00
1997	with 'U' in circle next to date	£1,800.00
1998	New portrait	£1,800.00
1999		£1,800.00
2000		£1,800.00
2000	with 'U' in circle next to date	£1,800.00
2001		£1,800.00
2002	Shield reverse	£1,800.00
2003 to 2010		£1,800.00
2011		£1,800.00
2012		£1,800.00
2013 to 2015		£1,800.00

Two Pounds (double sovereign)

All are cased proofs. The £2 coin has not often been issued on its own.

1987		£800.00
1988		£800.00
1989	Sovereign Anniversary type	£1,200.00
1990		£800.00
1991		£800.00
1992		£800.00
1993		£800.00
1994	(see 1994 error commemorative type 4 £2 coin)	
1996		£800.00
2014	In connection with birth of Prince George	£800.00

Sovereigns, loose bullion type

Sovereigns of the 1970s and 1980s are generally traded at their bullion value. They contain 7.32 grammes of fine gold. Particularly perfect examples may be worth a slight premium. The dates struck were as follows:

1974, 1976, 1978, 1979, 1980, 1981 and 1982	Bullion Value

Modern bullion type sovereigns, from 2000 to date, tend to sell for a little more than bullion value as follows (very new coins can sell for more):

	£320.00 to £340.00

Sovereigns, cased proof type

1979		£350.00
1980		£350.00
1981		£350.00
1982		£350.00
1983		£350.00
1984		£350.00
1985		£360.00
1986		£360.00
1987		£360.00
1988		£400.00
1989	500th Anniversary of the Sovereign reverse	£1,200.00
1990		£550.00
1991		£550.00
1992		£650.00
1993		£550.00
1994		£550.00
1995		£500.00
1996		£500.00
1997		£500.00
1998		£400.00
1999		£380.00
2000		£380.00
2001		£380.00
2002	Shield reverse	£380.00
2003		£380.00
2004		£380.00
2005 to 2013	(2005 and 2012 had alternate St. George reverses)	£400.00
2014* and 2015		£400.00
2016		£500.00
2017		£500.00

* Also reported with proof reverse and normal BU obverse.

Half Sovereigns, loose bullion type

Until recently, the 1982 Half Sovereign was the only non-proof coin and continues to trade at approximately bullion value. In 2000 the Royal Mint started issuing non-proof half sovereigns and have done so each year since. The 2000 to 2007 half sovereigns tend to trade from about £130 to £160 (based on the bullion value at the time of writing). The 1989 and 2002 shield reverse coins and the St. George 2005 coin are the most popular.

Half Sovereigns, cased proof type

1979		£170.00
1980		£170.00
1981		£170.00
1982		£170.00
1983		£170.00
1984		£170.00
1985		£170.00
1986		£170.00
1987		£170.00
1988		£170.00
1989	500th Anniversary of the Sovereign reverse	£350.00
1990		£170.00
1991		£170.00
1992		£170.00
1993		£170.00
1994		£170.00
1995		£170.00
1996		£170.00
1997		£170.00
1998		£170.00
1999		£170.00
2000		£170.00
2001		£180.00
2002	Shield reverse	£200.00
2003		£170.00
2004		£170.00
2005	Alternate St. George reverse	£190.00
2006		£170.00
2007		£170.00
2008 to 2013	(2012 had alternate St George reverse type)	£170.00
2014 and 2015		£180.00
2016 and 2017		£250.00
2017 and 2018		£300.00

Quarter Sovereigns

Introduced in 2009 as a made-up denomination (quarter of a sovereign is a crown, isn't it?) - they seem to sell for £90 - £150, both bullion and proof issue.

1980	10,000	£5, £2, Sovereign (£1), 1/2 Sovereign	£3,000.00
1981	-	Set containing 9 coins including silver Crown	no data
1982	2,500	£5, £2, Sovereign (£1), 1/2 Sovereign	£3,000.00
1983		£2, Sovereign (£1), 1/2 Sovereign	£1,400.00
1984	7,095	£5, Sovereign (£1), 1/2 Sovereign	£2,200.00
1985	5,849	£5, £2, Sovereign (£1), 1/2 Sovereign	£3000.00
1986	12,000	£2 Commonwealth Games, Sovereign (£1), 1/2 Sovereign	no data
1987	12,500	£2, Sovereign (£1), 1/2 Sovereign	£1,400.00
1988	12,500	£2, Sovereign (£1), 1/2 Sovereign	£1,500.00
1989	5,000	£5, £2, Sovereign (£1), 1/2 Sovereign (Anniversary reverse)	£4,000.00
	7,936	£2, Sovereign (£1), 1/2 Sovereign (Anniversary reverse)	£3,000.00
1990	1,721	£5, £2, Sovereign (£1), 1/2 Sovereign	£3,100.00
	1,937	£2, Sovereign (£1), 1/2 Sovereign	£1,400.00
1991	1,336	£5, £2, Sovereign (£1), 1/2 Sovereign	£3,100.00
	1,152	£2, Sovereign (£1), 1/2 Sovereign	£1,400.00
1992	1,165	£5, £2, Sovereign (£1), 1/2 Sovereign	£3,100.00
	967	£2, Sovereign (£1), 1/2 Sovereign	£1,400.00
1993	1,078	£5, £2, Sovereign (£1), 1/2 Sovereign (Pistrucci medallion)	£3,300.00
	663	£2, Sovereign (£1), 1/2 Sovereign	£1,500.00
1994	918	£5, £2 (Bank of England), Sovereign (£1), 1/2 Sovereign	£3,100.00
	1,249	£2 (Bank of England), Sovereign (£1), 1/2 Sovereign	£1,500.00
1995	718	£5, £2 (Dove of Peace), Sovereign (£1), 1/2 Sovereign	£3,100.00
	1,112	£2 (Dove of Peace), Sovereign (£1), 1/2 Sovereign	£1,500.00
1996	742	£5, £2, Sovereign (£1), 1/2 Sovereign	£3,100.00
	868	£2, Sovereign (£1), 1/2 Sovereign	£1,500.00
1997	860	£5, £2 (bi-metallic), Sovereign (£1), 1/2 Sovereign	£3,100.00
	817	£2 (bi-metallic), Sovereign (£1), 1/2 Sovereign	£1,500.00
1998	789	£5, £2, Sovereign (£1), 1/2 Sovereign	£3,100.00
	560	£2, Sovereign (£1), 1/2 Sovereign	£1,400.00
1999	991	£5, £2 (Rugby World Cup), Sovereign (£1), 1/2 Sovereign	£3,100.00
	912	£2 (Rugby World Cup), Sovereign (£1), 1/2 Sovereign	£1,500.00
2000	1,000	£5, £2, Sovereign (£1), 1/2 Sovereign	£3,200.00
	1,250	£2, Sovereign (£1), 1/2 Sovereign	£1,500.00

2017 Sovereign - a reproduced version of the original
sovereign reverse (1817 - 1820) was used to mark the
200th anniversary of the sovereign.

2001	1,000	£5, £2 (Marconi), Sovereign (£1), 1/2 Sovereign	£3,100.00
	891	£2 (Marconi), Sovereign (£1), 1/2 Sovereign	£1,400.00
2002	3,000	£5, £2, Sovereign (£1), 1/2 Sovereign (Shield reverse)	£3,100.00
	3,947	£2, Sovereign (£1), 1/2 Sovereign.(Shield reverse)	£1,500.00
2003	2,250	£5, £2, Sovereign (£1), 1/2 Sovereign	£3,300.00
	1,717	£2 (DNA), Sovereign (£1), 1/2 Sovereign	£1,400.00
2004	2,250	£5, £2, Sovereign (£1), 1/2 Sovereign	£3,100.00
	2,500	£2, £1 (Forth Bridge), 1/2 Sovereign	£1,400.00
2005	1,500	£5, £2, Sovereign (£1), 1/2 Sovereign	£3,100.00
	2,500	£2, Sovereign (£1), 1/2 Sovereign	£1,400.00
2006	1,750	£5, £2, Sovereign (£1), 1/2 Sovereign	£3,100.00
	1,750	£2, Sovereign (£1), 1/2 Sovereign	£1,500.00
2007		Sovereign, 1/2 Sovereign	£550.00
	700	£2, Sovereign, 1/2 Sovereign	£1,500.00
2008		Sovereign, 1/2 Sovereign	£550.00
		£5, £2, Sovereign, 1/2 Sovereign	£3,100.00
		£2, Sovereign, 1/2 Sovereign	£1,500.00
2009		£5, £2, Sovereign, 1/2 Sovereign and new 1/4 Sovereign	£3,100.00
		£2, Sovereign, 1/2 Sovereign and new 1/4 Sovereign	£1,400.00
2010		£5, £2, Sovereign, 1/2 Sovereign, 1/4 Sovereign. Issue price	£2,550.00
		Sovereign, 1/2 Sovereign, 1/4 Sovereign. Issue price	£550.00
		'Premium' set, 3 coins as above. Issue price	£1,030.00

Values of later sets are similar. They are a lot more expensive when bought new.

Based on a tradition dating back to the 12th century, every year on Maundy Thursday (the day before Good Friday), the monarch distributes leather pouches of special coins to selected people in a Royal Ceremony. The number of recipients is equal to the age of the monarch, as is the value of the coins in each pouch.

All Maundy coinage issued under the reign of Queen Elizabeth II carries the same obverse portrait, that of the first bust of the Queen used on coins and designed by Mary Gillick. On decimalisation day in 1971 the Maundy coins were re-valued from old pence to new pence.

Prices listed here are for complete sets in official Royal Mint cases, which became standard in the 1960s. Commencing in 1989, the coins are individually encapsulated within the case.

1971	1,018	Tewkesbury Abbey	£190.00
1972	1,026	York Minster	£200.00
1973	1,004	Westminster Abbey	£190.00
1974	1,042	Salisbury Cathedral	£190.00
1975	1,050	Peterborough Cathedral	£190.00
1976	1,158	Hereford Cathedral	£190.00
1977	1,138	Westminster Abbey	£190.00
1978	1,178	Carlisle Cathedral	£190.00
1979	1,188	Winchester Cathedral	£190.00
1980	1,198	Worcester Cathedral	£190.00
1981	1,178	Westminster Abbey	£190.00
1982	1,218	St. David's Cathedral, Dyfed	£190.00
1983	1,228	Exeter Cathedral	£190.00
1984	1,238	Southwell Minster	£190.00
1985	1,248	Ripon Cathedral	£190.00
1986	1,378	Chichester Cathedral	£150.00
1987	1,390	Ely Cathedral	£140.00
1988	1,402	Lichfield Cathedral	£140.00
1989	1,353	Birmingham Cathedral	£140.00
1990	1,523	Newcastle Cathedral	£140.00
1991	1,384	Westminster Abbey	£140.00
1992	1,424	Chester Cathedral	£140.00
1993	1,440	Wells Cathedral	£140.00
1994	1,433	Truro Cathedral	£140.00
1995	1,466	Coventry Cathedral	£150.00
1996	1,629	Norwich Cathedral	£150.00
1997	1,786	Bradford Cathedral	£150.00
1998	1,654	Portsmouth Cathedral	£150.00
1999	1,676	Bristol Cathedral	£150.00
2000	1,684	Lincoln Cathedral	£150.00
2000	13,180	silver proof set, (also included in the "Millennium Proof Set")	£150.00
2001	1,706	Westminster Abbey	£150.00
2002	1,678	Canterbury Cathedral	£150.00

2002	2,002	gold proof set, taken from special "Golden Jubilee Proof Set".	£1,100.00
2003		Gloucester Cathedral	£150.00
2004		Liverpool (Anglican) Cathedral	£150.00
2005		Wakefield Cathedral	£150.00
2006		Guildford Cathedral	£150.00
2007		Manchester Cathedral	
2008		St. Patrick's Cathedral, Armagh	
2009		St. Edmundsbury Cathedral, Suffolk	
2010		Derby Cathedral	
2011		Westminster Abbey	
2012		York Minster	
2013		Christ Church Cathedral, Oxford	
2014		Blackburn Cathedral	
2015		Sheffield Cathedral, South Yorkshire	
2016		St Georges Chapel, Windsor	
2017		Leicester Cathedral	
2018		St Georges Chapel, Windsor	
2019		St Georges Chapel, Windsor	
2020		Cancelled. Coins were sent out in the post.	

ERROR COINS

Error coins have always been very hard to value. It is true for any coin, but is particularly valid for most error coins, that they really are worth what someone is willing to pay for them, as by their very nature they are often unique. Other error types exist in larger numbers (e.g. the 2008 mule 20p, 1983 NEW PENCE 2p etc) and for those the demand for them sets the value.

See checkyourchange.co.uk for an introduction on error coins, the most comprehensive list of UK decimal error coins (over 350) with many images showing some quite extreme examples.

The Cover Image.

The image on the cover of this book shows the Jody Clark fifth portrait of the Queen, which was introduced in March 2015. In the background are some faint images of recent coin reverses, from the top, clockwise: the 2020 George III £5 coin, to mark 200 years since the end of his reign, the Team GB 2020 (that will now be held in 2021) Olympics 50p, 2019 Wallace & Gromit 50p, 2020 Agatha Christie £2, 2020 Mayflower £2 and the 2020 D-Day £2.